The Ultimate Instant Cookbook

Fresh and Foolproof Instant Pot/Electric Pressure Cooker Recipes for Beginners and Advanced Users

Jason Rowley

Instant Pot Ultra
www.InstantPot.com
Pressure Cook
Soup/Broth
Meat/Stew
Bean/Chili
Steam
Slow Cook
Sauté
Warm
Rice
Porridge
Multigrain
Cake
Egg
Sterilize
Yogurt
Ultra
Cancel
Start

Table of Contents

INTRODUCTION 9

CHAPTER 1: THE BENEFITS OF INSTANT POT 11
- Using the Instant pot pressure cooker/Beginners guide 13
- Methods of cooking and Electric Pressure Cooker Functions 16
- Cleaning and caring for your electric pressure cooker 19

CHAPTER 2: BREAKFAST RECIPES 21
- Recipe 1: Mixed Fried Vegetables with Indian Spices 22
- Recipe 2: French toast With Blueberries 24
- Recipe 3: Grits and Bacon Breakfast 26
- Recipe 4: Instant Pot Yogurt Breakfast 28
- Recipe 5: Nuts Granola with Raisins 30
- Recipe 6: Hash Brown Bake 32
- Recipe 7: Scottish Eggs 34
- Recipe 8: Instant Pot Breakfast Quiche 36
- Recipe 9: Quinoa with Fruits 38
- Recipe 10: Potato Frittata 39
- Recipe 11: Mashed Potatoes with Scrambled Eggs 41
- Recipe 12: Egg Muffins 43
- Recipe 13: Eggs with Mushrooms and Ham 45

CHAPTER 3: RICE AND PASTA RECIPE 47
- Recipe 14: Rice curry with Lamb 48
- Recipe 15: Hawaiian-Style Rice with Beef 50
- Recipe 16: Cajun Rice 52
- Recipe 17: Cajun Rice 54
- Recipe 18: Jasmine Rice With veggies 56
- Recipe 19: Rice Pilaf with Fennel 57
- Recipe 20: Long-Grain Rice with cranberries 59
- Recipe 21: Rice with Cilantro and spinach 61
- Recipe 22: Rice with Cashews 63
- Recipe 23: Rice with avocado 65
- Recipe 24: Rice with Lentils and Peas 66
- Recipe 25: Spicy White Rice with Chili and Cumin 68
- Recipe 26: Rice with black Beans 70
- Recipe 27: Sweet Potato Coconut Rice 72
- Recipe 28: Shrimp Scampi 74
- Recipe 29: Bruschetta Chicken Pasta 76

CHAPTER 4: VEGETABLES, GRAINS AND BEANS RECIPES 78
- Recipe 30: Vegetables Medley Instant Pot 79

- Recipe 31: Instant Pot Pinto Beans...........81
- Recipe 32: Lentil Spicy Gumbo...........83
- Recipe 33: Instant Pot Red beans...........85
- Recipe 34: Instant Pot Spicy Chickpeas with Cumin...........87
- Recipe 35: Spicy Quinoa Chili...........89
- Recipe 36: Cauliflower Curry...........91
- Recipe 37: Pumpkin Curry...........93
- Recipe 38: Veggie Falafel...........94
- Recipe 39: Stuffed Peppers...........96
- Recipe 40: Stuffed Mushrooms...........98
- Recipe 41: Stuffed Cabbage...........99
- Recipe 42: Instant Pot Hummus...........101

CHAPTER 5: SOUPS AND STEWS RECIPES...........102

- Recipe 43: Butternut squash soup...........103
- Recipe 44: Chicken Soup...........105
- Recipe 45: Chicken Curry Soup...........107
- Recipe 46: Asparagus Soup...........109
- Recipe 47: Lentil Soup...........111
- Recipe 48: Potato Soup...........113
- Recipe 49: Cauliflower Soup...........115
- Recipe 50: Carrot soup with fowl...........117
- Recipe 51: Instant Pot Angel Hair Soup...........119
- Recipe 52: Coconut Lime Soup...........121
- Recipe 53: Garlic Soup with Almonds...........123
- Recipe 54: Beef Noodle Soup...........125
- Recipe 55: Lamb Stew...........127

CHAPTER 6: SEAFOOD AND POULTRY RECIPES...........128

- Recipe 56: Salmon with mango salsa...........129
- Recipe 57: Salmon with Lemon Wedges...........131
- Recipe 58: Salmon with asparagus...........133
- Recipe 59: Shrimp with Mango...........135
- Recipe 60: Shrimp Dumplings...........137
- Recipe 61: Tilapia with Lemon slices...........139
- Recipe 62: Fish with Celery and Potatoes...........140
- Recipe 63: Fish with Strawberries and Kiwi...........142
- Recipe 64: Halibut with Blueberries...........144
- Recipe 65: Scallops with Strawberry Salsa...........146
- Recipe 66: Mahi Mahi with avocado Salsa...........148
- Recipe 67: Haddock Fish with Sweet Potatoes...........150
- Recipe 68: Swordfish with Herbs and Pineapple salsa...........152
- Recipe 69: Cod Fish with cauliflower Rice...........154
- Recipe 70: Cod Fish with cauliflower Rice...........156

- Recipe 71: Salmon with basil and dill 158
- Recipe 72: Seafood Gumbo 160
- Recipe 73: Shrimp Paella 162

Chapter 7: Beef, Lamb and Pork Recipes 164

- Recipe 74: Braised Pork 165
- Recipe 75: Instant Pot Ground meat casserole 167
- Recipe 76: Instant Pot Short Beef Ribs 169
- Recipe 77: Instant Pot Beef Liver 171
- Recipe 78: Instant Pot Beef roast 173
- Recipe 79: Pulled pork 175
- Recipe 80: Pork with Pineapple 177
- Recipe 81: Balsamic Pork 179
- Recipe 82: Pork Tagine 180
- Recipe 83: Instant Pot Pork Belly 182
- Recipe 84: Spinach Stuffed Beef Rolls 184
- Recipe 85: Pulled Beef 186
- Recipe 86: Instant Pot Pork Tenderloin 188
- Recipe 87: Pork with dates 190
- Recipe 88: Pork with mushrooms 192

Chapter 8: Turkey, Goose and Duck Recipes 194

- Recipe 89: Instant Pot Duck Breast 195
- Recipe 90: Middle Eastern-Style Turkey 197
- Recipe 91: Orange Turkey 199
- Recipe 92: Stuffed Turkey breast 201
- Recipe 93: Turkey Meatballs with tomato sauce 203
- Recipe 94: Turkey meatloaf 205
- Recipe 95: Turkey Chili 207
- Recipe 96: Curried Ground Turkey 209
- Recipe 97: Ground Turkey with Peppers 211
- Recipe 98: Turkey Burgers 213
- Recipe 99: Quinoa Bowl 215

Chapter 9: Stocks and Sauces Recipes 217

- Recipe 100: Spaghetti Sauce 218
- Recipe 101: Chicken Stock 220
- Recipe 102: Bolognese sauce 222
- Recipe 103: Cream Béchamel 224
- Recipe 104: Mornay Sauce 226
- Recipe 105: Mushroom Sauce 228
- Recipe 106: Custard Sauce 230
- Recipe 107: Chocolate Sauce 232
- Recipe 108: Mexican-Style Barbecue Sauce 233
- Recipe 109: Mexican-Style Barbecue Sauce 235

- Recipe 110: Espagnole Sauce 237
- Recipe 111: Enchilada Sauce 239
- Recipe 112: Bordelaise Sauce 241
- Recipe 113: Spicy Indian Sauce 243
- Recipe 114: Sweet Red Chili Sauce 245
- Recipe 115: Alfredo Sauce 247

Chapter 116: Desserts and Bread Recipes 249

- Recipe 117: Cheese Cake 250
- Recipe 118: Chocolate Cookies 252
- Recipe 119: Brownie Cake 254
- Recipe 120: Coconut Custard 256
- Recipe 121: Chocolate Mousse 258
- Recipe 123: Strawberry Compote 260
- Recipe 124: Instant Pot Flan 261
- Recipe 125: Chocolate Cupcakes 263
- Recipe 126: Chocolate Chip Cake 265
- Recipe 127: Pear Compote 267
- Recipe 128: Strawberry Mousse 269
- Recipe 129: Crème Brule 271
- Recipe 130: Sweet Cinnamon Almonds 273
- Recipe 131: Apple Cinnamon Rolls 275
- Recipe 132: Pecan Pie 277
- Recipe 133: Lava Cake 279

Conclusion 281

© Copyright 2020 By Jason Rowley All Right Reserved.

In no way it is legal to reproduce, duplicate, or transmit any part of this document by other electronic means or printed format. Any recording of this publication is strictly prohibited, and any storage of this material is not allowed unless with a written permission from the publisher. All rights reserved.

The information provided herein is stated to be truthful and consistent, in that any liability, regarding inattention or otherwise, by any use or abuse of any policies, processes, or directions contained within is the solitary and complete responsibility of the recipient reader. Under no circumstances will any legal liability or blame be held against the publisher for any reparation, damages, or monetary loss due to the information herein, either directly or indirectly.

Legal Notice:

This book is copyright protected. This is only for personal use. You cannot amend, distribute, sell, use, quote or paraphrase any part or the content within this book without the consent of the author or copyright owner. Legal action will be pursued if it is breached

DISCLAIMER NOTICE:

Please only read the information contained within this document is for educational purposes only. Every attempt has been made to provide accurate, up to date, complete and reliable information. No warranties of any kind are expressed or implied. Readers acknowledge that the author is not engaged in the rendering of legal, financial, medical or professional advice.

By reading this document, the reader agrees that under no circumstances are we responsible for any losses, direct or indirect, which are incurred as a result of the use of information contained in this document, including but not limited to errors, omissions, or any inaccuracies

Introduction

Are you busy and all the time on the run all the time that you can't even cook your favorite your favorite dishes and healthy meals? Do you frequently have to overcook or undercook your dishes because you are under pressure every day? If yes, then pressure cooking will be the perfect solution for all your cooking problems and this cookbook is the perfect place where you can start from.

For instance, Electric pressure cookers and instant pots have become incredibly popular and widely used over the years because for they ingeniously combine a wide variety of features into just one appliance. And while it is categorized as Electric Pressure cooker, any Instant Pot is considered as a 7-in-1 programmable cooker that have the different functions of slow cooker, pressure cooker, steamer, rice cooker, yogurt maker, sauté pan and even a warmer and this is all in one appliance.

Furthermore, Instant Pots also feature built-in smart programs, therefore, only with the push of one button; you can easily come up with a delicious pot of stew or porridge. And with its sleek and unique design, Instant Pots take up very little space on the counter, which makes it an ideal appliance for everyone of us, including condo dwellers and even students. And on this framework, we offer you this Ultimate Instant Pot cookbook in which you will learn all the skills you need to use Instant Pots, Electric Pressure cookers.

Instant pot recipes are indeed a natural way that can help us take a step back from our beloved yet conventional cooking tools and utensils, like crock pots and offer us the opportunity to enjoy our cooking experience through trying the method of pressure cooking, but in a modern way. Instant pots, Electric pressure cookers will help you the joy of pressure cooking. And the electric pressure cookers of today have become more considered as a fast version of slow cookers, but with no cooking risks at all.

So, if you are looking for a cooking method that will make you cook at ease and never worry about burning your foods, meats or dishes; and whether you want to invest your precious time or offer this cookbook to your dear ones, there is no better choice to make than this cookbook. Digging into the deep past, the use of pressure cooking has existed for centuries, but it wasn't until the recent times that the electric pressure cooking method has revolutionized the whole cooking process and experience as a whole.

Only with pressure cooking, you will be able to transform chewy, cheap, cuts of meat into tender masterpieces, fruits, veggies and grains much faster than ever before. The use of healthy Electric Pressure cooking will help you get the nutrients out of the used ingredients easier, faster and more delicious than ever before. And with the help of Instant Pots, you will never have to order pizza or hamburger after a long day at work.

This Instant Pot Electric pressure cooker cookbook includes all of the major pieces of information that are needed to help you feel confident with the use of electric pressure cooker, even if it is your first use of pressure cooker. And before jumping to the recipes, you important introductory information needed to feel comfortable and confident with an electric pressure cooker, even if it's your first time using one. In just the first few chapters of this cookbook, you will learn everything you need to know about:

- Benefits of Instant Pot Electric Pressure Cookers
- The tips and use of electric pressure cookers
- Methods of cooking with Electric pressure cookers
- How to clean and take care of your Instant Pot Electric Pressure Cookers

After learning the various basics of the use of Instant Pots, electric Pressure cookers, you will find 250 sumptuous recipes, including breakfasts, rice and pasta, vegetable, grains and beans, beef, lamb, pork, turkey, duck, stocks, sauces and even desserts. The Instant Pot, Electric Pressure Cooker is perhaps considered as one of the most versatile cooking appliances in the whole world. And whether you are a New Instant Pot user or pro, this cooking guide is for you.

No matter how old you are, a beginner or a professional cook, and wherever you are, there is always something for you in this cookbook; so what are you waiting for to get started?

Chapter 1: The Benefits of Instant pot

Instant pots are very well-known for having a wide variety of uses and cooking methods which can make the use of this cooking appliance really easy and simple for us to use at home. But, not all instant pots are created in the same way; there are different brands of electric pressure cookers and each has a different functionality. And before using Instant Pots, you should first get to know the various benefits and advantages of Electric Pressure Cookers.

1. Saving Time & Energy

Instant Pots Electric pressure cookers are characterized by being energy efficient cooking appliances and they are second to microwaves in terms of use. And there are two major causes that may contribute to the Instant Pot efficiency in energy:

- A cooking chamber; every Instant Pot is equipped with an inner pot that is known as a cooking chamber and this inner pot is completely insulated. Therefore, Electric Pressure cookers don't need to export any type of energy in order to heat up.
- Electric Pressure cookers require less quantity of liquid that any traditional cooking method as it will boil faster. And compared to different conventional cookers or other cooking methods; like boiling, steaming, pressure cooking or baking may importantly reduce the cooking time as well as energy by about 70%.

2. Instant Pots can help preserve the taste of food and maintain its appearance

Usually cooking in open containers can lead to exposing your food to heat and oxygen; which may lead to diminished flavors. And pressure cooking usually saturates your food with steam, which allows the foods to retain bright colors and photochemical. Indeed, the airtight design can enable the flavors to be cooked faster and in a more profound way.

3. Electric Pressure Cookers Retrain Nutrients and Vitamins

Boiling, just like steaming can cause vitamins and nutrients to leech out of your food ingredients. Yet, electric pressure cookers can greatly help you cook food very quickly, evenly and really deeply. Besides, using an Electric Pressure Cooker can help retain more nutrients and nutritional element. Indeed, electric pressure cookers can retain up to about 90% of water.

4. Instant Pots can eliminate various Harmful Microorganisms

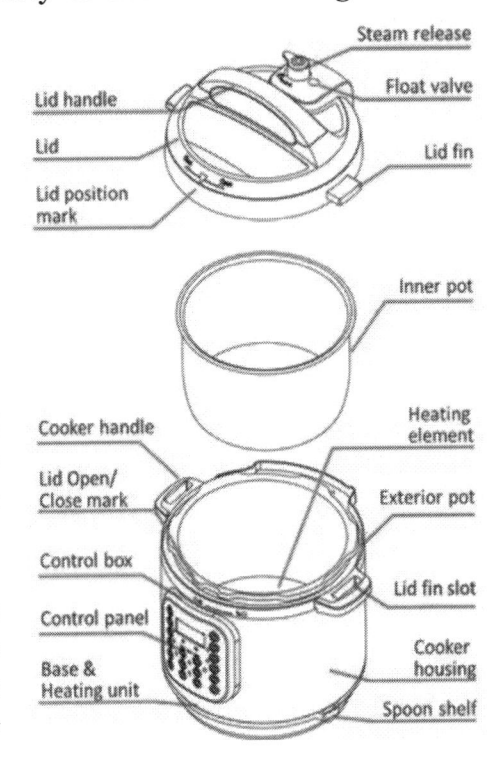

Using Electric Pressure cookers creates a cooking environment that allows water to boil higher than around 212°F. Electric Pressure Cookers are unique and very special for its ability to destroy and get rid completely of harmful bacteria. You can also use Instant Pots as a sterilization tool for baby bottles or jars or also for treating water.

5. It Is Safe To Use

Many people may get frustrated and really nervous when they hear the term pressure cooker; however, when using Electric Pressure Cookers is safer than you can imagine. Instant pots display an automatic lid lock as well as a lid detection that can make it impossible to open up the lid before all the pressure in your instant pot has been released. Besides, Instant pots come with an automation automatic temperature control system and that can keep the temperature inside the Electric Pressure Cooker in a safe level all the time.

6. Instant Pots are Easy To Clean

In addition to being fast at cooking and efficient, instant pots are also characterized by being easy to clean. All you have to do when using Instant Pots is to wash the inner pot. Then after cleaning the Instant Pot; clean its silicone ring and the lid too. It is also advisable that you repeat the same cleaning process every time you use your instant pot.

Using the Instant pot pressure cooker/Beginners guide

Electric Pressure cookers can save you time and money, and helping you prepare a wide variety of delicious meals; Instant Pots are super easy to use, if you know some very simple basics. Indeed, pressure cooking needs no more than some tips; adjustments and techniques for the best cooking results. And here are some of the most useful pressure cooking tips that can help you through your pressure cooking journey:

1. Be careful not to overdo the liquid:

Because cooking food in a closed Instant Pot, sealed under pressure; you will have less evaporation and you should therefore pay attention to the quantity of liquid that you should use while pressure cooking in comparison to conventional cooking pots. And regardless of any dish or meal you are cooking; make sure to use enough liquid for your food ingredients. And usually, there is a general rule that a thumb approximately equals 1 cup of liquid. And in general never fill the Electric Pressure cooker more than half of it with the liquid.

2. Don't overcrowd your Instant Pot with too much food ingredients.

Never fill your Electric Pressure cookers with two-thirds full of ingredients. Besides, never try to pack food into your Instant Pot. And if you don't follow this top and basics; the pressure cooking process won't be successful and won't operate in an efficient way. By overcrowding the Electric Pressure Cooker, you can also cause the safety valves to activate.

3. Always make sure to use even pieces

Remember that to come up with the best pressure cooking cooked food needs using even pieces of ingredients. Therefore, you should always use pieces of food that are cut into pieces of the same size so that they will be cooked in the same amount of time.

4. Start off high and finish up low. When cooking in a stove-top pressure cooker, start cooking over high heat. After you reach pressure, lower the burner to a simmer. No need to worry about adjusting the heat when cooking in an electric pressure cooker. The appliance does it for you automatically.

5. **Always set a timer:**

Always make sure to have a kitchen timer handy to help your electric pressure cooker reach the perfect heat and maintain pressure. And note that all types of electric pressure cookers are equipped with digital timers built in.

6. **To use an electric pressure cooker is very easy:**

All you have to do is to choose your desired pressure level through pressing either the low or the high pressure button on the control pan. Then set the time you need to cook your recipe; then press the button start. And when the timer beeps; it indicates that the cooking process is done and your food is ready. When the pressure is released; you can use a quick release pressure method or a natural releasing method

7. Always make sure never to attempt a cold-water release method with your Instant Pot Electric Pressure cooker. And unless you want to shorten the lifespan of your Instant Pot; never submerge your cooking appliance into water. And always make sure to unplug the instant pot before cleaning it.

8. Generally speaking, the time that takes your Instant Pot to depressurize depends on various reasons; like the heating process, which can take from about 5 to 40 minutes. Frozen or cold foods may increase the amount of pressure cooking time. And all the terms and the cooking times are interchangeable.

9. Some types of food, like cranberries, pearl barley, split peas, oatmeal and noodles may cause the steam release pipe. So you need to pay extreme caution and attention while using these types of ingredients.

10. Always make sure to keep two Instant Pot sealing rings on hand to use for your savory dishes and one for your sweet dishes.

11. If you want to cook pasta with your Electric Pressure cooker, it is better to use dry noodles that have a cooking time of about 8 minutes. Submerge the pasta if it is possible, but don't stir it.

12. It is okay to use the steam rack to help lift the foods out of your cooking liquid. And the use of rack will ensure an even distribution of heat; and can prevent the nutrients from leeching out of your cooking liquid. The use of rack can also stop any burning risk on the bottom of the inner pot of the Instant Pot.

13. Usually, all the programs except for the Rice default to a High Pressure while for the Rice; the default is a Low Pressure. And for the best rice results; it is better to leave the lid on after the cooking cycle ends for an additional 5 to 10 minutes before using the quick releasing pressure.

14. When pressure cooking any dish; always make sure to steam the release handle/valve or to apply a quick release button is while in the "Sealing" position.

15. The pressure cooking liquids that are usually used should be water-based, like stock, juice or broth.

Methods of cooking and Electric Pressure Cooker Functions

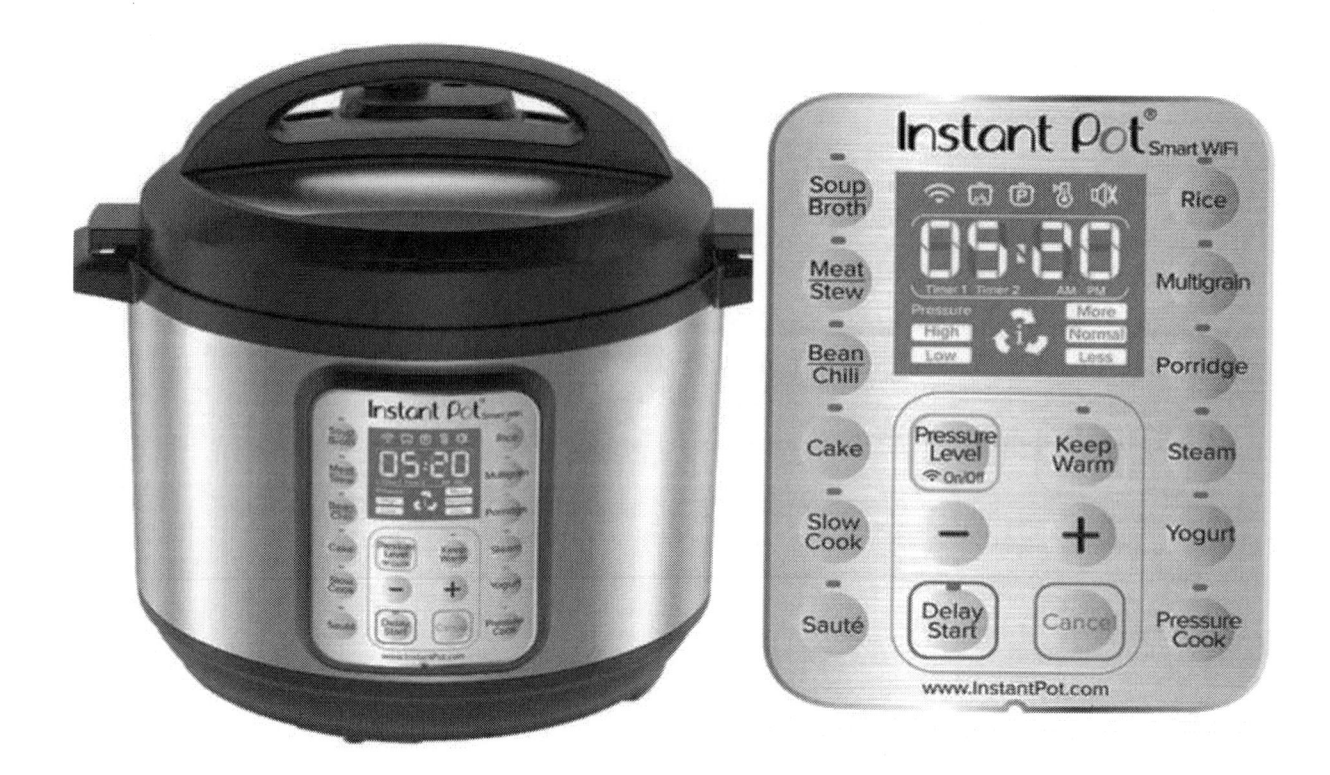

Instant Pots can make your life super easy and the use of Instant Pots can make it possible for you to make your life much easier. Indeed, Instant Pots make it possible for you to use it only through chucking a few ingredients in your Electric Pressure Cooker. Then to use an Instant Pot; all you have to do is to press a button, and you will get your meal in a very short time.

And if you want to enjoy some of the most delicious meals that you can ever taste; there are a very few things that you can do to make and Instant Pot function better. Therefore, if you are an owner of an Instant Pot, Electric Pressure cooker; you should learn about its various uses; and functions. And you will probably start relying more on this cooking appliance after you learn about its uses and versatility.

Indeed, there are some of the most important uses of Instant Pot Pressure Cooker:

1. Slow cooker
2. Rice Cooker
3. Pressure cooker
4. Steamer
5. Yogurt maker
6. Saute/browning
7. Warmer

And here are the major settings you can find in any Instant Pot:

- **The MANUAL/PRESSURE COOK SETTING:**

The pressure or manual cook setting can allow you to set the cooking time to whatever time you want. And this is by far one of the most used functions that you can use on your Instant Pot, because once you are just setting a specific time; it means that you are in total control of the pressure cooking process.

- **To Use the Manual Button:**

Hit the Manual; then hit the pressure button until you get a low or high pressure and if you want to adjust the pressure; just adjust it manually by pressing the button; then hit the minus or plus signs to adjust the time.

- **The Sauté Function**

This function is greatly known browning vegetables, meat or for thickening up any sauce at the end of pressure cooking. You can also use this function for your Instant Pot Mongolian Beef and for Instant Pot Chili. And to use the sauté function; all you have to do is to press the "sauté" button.

- Select the temperature you need to through using the key "Adjust" for "Normal", "Less" or you can use "more".
- When your Instant Pot reaches the desired temperature, it will display "Hot" and then you may start sautéing.
- The full "Sauté" process will run for about 30 minutes.
- The Normal heat of the Instant Pot is like high heat on the top of stove and less is like low heat on a stove top.

- **Yogurt button:**

The function yogurt is only used only for making yogurt. And generally speaking, the yogurt button can be adjusted by hitting the adjust button until it displays "Boil" or about 8:00 or about 10:00. And these functions are all specific to yogurt recipes and making yogurt. So if you plan to make yogurt in your Instant Pot, you should use the Yogurt Setting.

- **The pressure setting**

This specific function allows you to adjust the pressure for high or for low—not and it is an option that is rarely used. Most of the recipes are generally designed to be cooked on high pressure than a low pressure. Yet, it is also important to pay great attention to this because if you accidently hot a button causing the pressure to drop from high to low; this will affect the obtained food may be damaged.

- **To use the Pressure Button**: All you have to do is to hit the pressure button; and after hitting the pressure button; you need to adjust it to a high or low pressure.
- Set the timer on for a manual cooking as needed.
- **Adjust the button:** To adjust the button means to adjust the temperature of your Instant Pot when you choose the cooking function.

To adjust the button is to adjust the temperature of the instant pot when using the slow cooking, yogurt, or sauté functions between less, normal, and more.

- **The Timer button**

The timer function is used to delay the cooking time in general. And this is great for example when you make Instant Pot oats or brown rice. And you can also prepare the rice in the morning; then set it to be ready at dinner or prepare oats and then you will wake up to enjoy the delicious taste of oatmeal. And the second thing that you should keep in mind while you use an instant pot is that you are setting the timer as to when you want to start cooking your recipes. And the delay start, generally doesn't count until the Electric pressure cooker comes to pressure.

- **To Use the Timer Function:**

Select either the manual pressure cooking or the slow cooker mode; because both of these are considered as the two compatible modes with the timer function. Set your timer and only within 10 seconds of setting the cooking time; just press the timer button. Then use the "+/-" keys to set the delay time.

- **The slow cooker button**

The Instant Pot Slow Cooker function is not usually equivalent to the temperatures on a conventional slow cooker. And Electric Pressure cookers doesn't work like any regular slow cooker.

- **Other instant pot buttons**

Depending on the type of the Instant Pot and the model you have; you may have various settings for cooking meat; including settings for chicken, meat, eggs, rice, stew or soup, and cake. It is also better to cook on low or high pressure and to manually adjust the temperature you yourself based on what you are cooking.

Cleaning and caring for your electric pressure cooker

If you own an Electric Pressure Cooker; you should know that having such a cooking appliance is an asset itself. Not only Electric Pressure Cookers can save your time and energy; but it can help you benefit as much as possible from different nutrients and flavors. But in order to keep your Instant Pot always safe-to use, you should know the perfect way that can help you clean your cooking appliance:

Cleaning your Instant Pot Electric Cooker

- To be able to properly use your Instant Pot, you should know how to clean it first of all after every use. For example, leaving food residues in your Instant Pot can greatly ruin the lifespan of this cooking appliance. And leaving food residues in your Instant Pot for a long period of time may cause indentations within the metal of your cooking appliance.

- You can also use a dishwasher for cleaning your Instant Pot, Electric Pressure cooker, but only if your Electric Pressure is dishwasher safe. And always make sure to read the instruction manual to make sure if the dishwasher is safe.

- To wash Instant Pot, you can start by separating all of its parts; the lid, the gasket, the pressure weight and the pot separately with a sponge, the water and the mild dishwashing soap. You should also take special care while you choose to wash the gasket for you not to risk deforming it.

- If you want to remove any dried food that is stuck inside your electric pressure cooker; just add one cup of water with some of the dishing washing liquid and cook on a low flame without locking it with a lid. And as the water starts to boil, the food residue will start to come off. Then turn the flame and wash following the same way.

- If you want to clean a burnt Instant Pot, fill it half way; then add a few layers of onion and let cook without the lid for about 20 minutes before turning off the heat. Wash in the usual way; and the burnt food will come off easily.

Storing your Instant Pot

- To store your Instant Pot Electric Pressure cooker; you should first make sure it is completely dry so that you prevent any bacterial growth. And after the Instant Pot has completely dried, you can store it in a clean and dry place.
- Furthermore, for further security against moisture and bacteria, you can sprinkle a little quantity of baking soda inside it on the walls and on the base. And this will also keep your Instant Pot free of any foods.
- If your Electric Pressure cooker is of a small size, you can store it inside an airtight jar.
- Store your Instant with the gasket fitted with into the lid and the lid place upside down over the Electric Pressure Cooker. And if you seal the lid on the Electric Pressure Cooker while you store it; the odors of the food will be preserved and this will have an effect on the meat you will cook the next time.
- To assure a perfect maintenance of your Instant Pot, Electric Pressure Cooker, you should remember to give an inspection to your electric Pressure Cooker every about 5 to 6 months.
- Remember to keep a close check on the knobs, the gasket and the handle of the Electric Pressure Cooker to loosen any possible damage. You will also need to replace any part that can be damaged.
- Generally speaking, it is considered a good idea to replace the gasket at least once per year because it can become loose with time. And if the gasket is loose, you may not notice that while you are cooking. In this case; the liquid will start to boil; then evaporate it if you are not supervising the cooking process.
- For older models of pressure cookers that come with a pressure weight, ensure that there are no residues that are left stuck inside it; left stuck inside it; you can also clear the path with a needle or a toothpick.
- Tighten the handle and the screws if they become a bit loose and grease the handle with a little quantity of oil to improve the performance.

CHAPTER 2: BREAKFAST RECIPES

Recipe 1: Mixed Fried Vegetables with Indian Spices

TIME TO PREPARE
10 minutes

COOK TIME
20 minutes

SERVING
3 People

Ingredients

- 2 Cups of steel cut oats
- 2 Cups of milk
- 1 Cups of yogurt
- 3 Cups of water
- 4 Diced apples
- 1 and ½ cups of fresh cranberries
- 2 to 4 tablespoons of virgin coconut oil
- 1 Teaspoon of fresh lemon juice
- 1 Teaspoon of cinnamon
- ½ Teaspoon of nutmeg
- ¼ Cup of maple syrup
- ½ Teaspoon of salt
- 2 Teaspoons of vanilla

Instructions

1. Start by greasing your Instant Pot with a little bit of coconut oil
2. Soak all your ingredients except for the maple syrup, the salt and the vanilla for an overnight in your Instant Pot
3. Add the salt and the maple syrup; then press the setting 'Porridge' and seal the valve
4. It will take about 20 minutes for the pressure to get up and about 20 minutes to be ready
5. When the timer beeps; quick release the pressure; then open the lid
6. Add in the vanilla
7. Serve your breakfast with milk and enjoy its taste!

Nutrition Information

Calories: 200.1, Fat: 8g, Carbohydrates: 26g, Dietary Fiber: 3 g, Protein: 15.2g

RECIPE 2: FRENCH TOAST WITH BLUEBERRIES

TIME TO PREPARE
9 minutes

COOK TIME
15 Minutes

SERVING
5 People

Ingredients

- 3 Large eggs
- 1 Cup of half and half cream
- ½ Cup of milk
- 1 Tablespoon of cinnamon
- 1 Teaspoon of vanilla
- 1 loaf of cubed, French bread
- ½ Cup of blueberries

Instructions

1. Spray the bottom of your Instant Pot with cooking spray
2. Dice the bread into cubes; then place it into your Instant Pot
3. Whisk altogether the milk, the cream, the cinnamon, the vanilla and the eggs
4. Pour the mixture of custard over the cubes of the bread and coat it very well
5. Sprinkle the bread with the blueberries
6. Lock the lid of your Instant Pot; then seal the valve
7. Set the timer to about 15 minutes and the pressure to high
8. When the timer beeps; quick release the pressure; then open the lid
9. Serve and enjoy your French toast with blueberries!

Nutrition Information

Calories: 252, Fat: 15g, Carbohydrates: 21.5g, Dietary Fiber: 3.7 g, Protein: 14g

Recipe 3: Grits and Bacon Breakfast

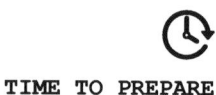

TIME TO PREPARE
5 minutes

COOK TIME
10 Minutes

SERVING
3 People

Ingredients

- ¼ Cup of Stone Ground Grits
- ½ Cup of Water
- ½ Cup of milk
- 2 Teaspoons of Bacon Grease
- 1 Cup of Cheddar Cheese
- ½ Teaspoon of salt
- 1 Cup of water
- A little bit of Butter for garnishing

Instructions

1. Place all of your ingredients into a heat-proof baking bowl
2. Pour 1 cup of water into your Instant Pot
3. Place the trivet in its place in the bottom of your Instant Pot
4. Place the heat proof bowl with the ingredients over the top of your trivet
5. Lock the lid of your Instant Pot and set the timer to about 10 minutes and the pressure to HIGH
6. When the timer beeps; quick release the pressure; then press the button sauté and let the oil heat
7. Add the grits and toast it for about 3 minutes
8. When the timer beeps; turn off your instant pot and add the remaining ingredients
9. Close the lid of your Instant Pot and set at HIGH pressure for about 5 to 6 minutes
10. When the timer beeps; quick release the pressure and open the pressure valve in order to release the remaining pressure

11. Serve and enjoy your breakfast!

Nutrition Information

Calories: 210.4, Fat: 15.4g, Carbohydrates: 6g, Dietary Fiber: 0.1 g, Protein: 12.4g

Recipe 4: Instant Pot Yogurt Breakfast

TIME TO PREPARE
10 minutes

COOK TIME
8 Hours

SERVING
5 People

Ingredients

- 52 Ounces of Ultra-Pasteurized Milk
- 1 Tablespoon of Fresh Yogurt live cultures

Instructions

1. Start by cleaning your Instant Pot
2. Pour the milk in your Instant Pot; then add about 1 tablespoon of the yogurt to your Instant Pot
3. Whisk your ingredients very well together; then lock the lid of your Instant Pot
4. Press the button 'Yogurt' and use the buttons +/- in order to set the time for about 8 hours; then make sure the Yogurt setting displays Normal
5. When the timer beeps and the yogurt cycle is over; turn off your Instant Pot and remove the inner pot
6. Place your yogurt in the refrigerator to chill for an overnight
7. Serve and enjoy your yogurt with slices of strawberries!

Nutrition Information

Calories: 220, Fat: 11g, Carbohydrates: 9g, Dietary Fiber: 0 g, Protein: 20g

Recipe 5: Nuts Granola with Raisins

TIME TO PREPARE
5 minutes

COOK TIME
5 Minutes

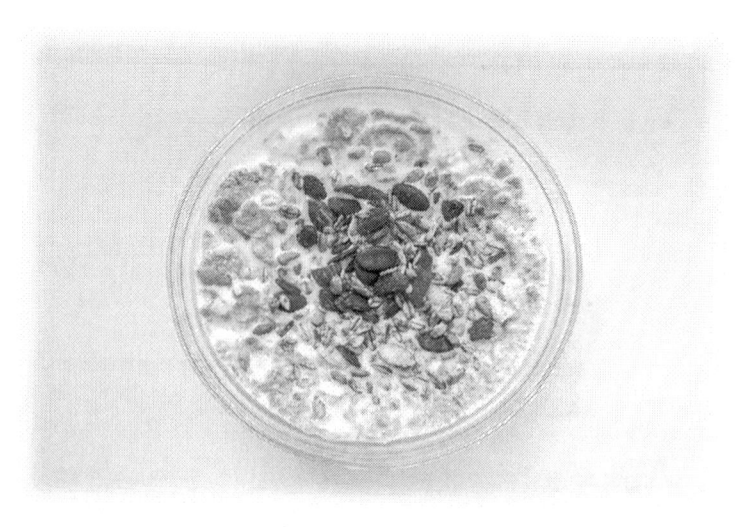

SERVING
4 People

Ingredients

- 3 Cups of oats
- 1 Cup of mixed nuts including
- ½ Cup of macadamia
- ½ Cup of sesame seeds
- ½ Cup of sunflower seeds
- ½ Cup of raisins
- ½ Cup of dried cranberries
- 1 Cup of chopped dried apricots
- 1 Cup of semi-skimmed milk
- Chopped pears
- Chopped, grapes, Papaya, pineapple and banana

Instructions

1. Turn on your Instant Pot and press the button sauté
2. Toss in the oats; the seeds, the raisins, the cranberries and the nuts
3. Add in the milk and lock the lid of your Instant Pot
4. Set the timer to about 5 minutes and the pressure to HIGH
5. When the time is up; quick release the pressure; then add in the apricots
6. Serve and enjoy your muesli with chopped fruits!

Nutrition Information

Calories: 260, Fat: 13g, Carbohydrates: 31g, Dietary Fiber: 3 g, Protein: 5g

Recipe 6: Hash Brown Bake

TIME TO PREPARE
6 minutes

COOK TIME
20 Minutes

SERVING
4-5 People

Ingredients

- 1 lb of breakfast pork sausage
- 1 Can of 4 oz of diced green chiles
- 3 Cups of shredded hash browns
- 8 Large eggs
- 1 Cup of cottage cheese
- 1/3 Cup of milk
- 1 and ½ cups of shredded Cheddar cheese
- 1 Pinch of salt and 1 pinch of pepper, to taste

Instructions

1. Start by turning your Instant Pot to the function, "sauté"
2. Spray the inner cavity of your Instant Pot with cooking spray.
3. When the Instant Pot heats up; add in the chopped chiles and the sausage.
4. Break up the sausage and cook it until it becomes no longer pink
5. Spoon out any extra of grease and in the meantime; whisk all together the milk, the eggs, the cottage cheese, thee salt and the pepper; then set it aside
6. Now; add in the hash browns and stir while cooking for about 2 additional minutes
7. Turn off the sauté function; and if you notice any brown bits on the bottom of your instant pot; remove the mixture of the hash browns and the sausage; then scrape off the Instant Pot and clean the bottom
8. Pour the mixture of the egg on top of the sausage, hash browns and chile combination
9. Make sure the potatoes are covered very well

32

10. Top with the shredded cheese
11. Turn the Instant Pot to Manual and set for about 20 minutes
12. When the time is up; turn off the Instant Pot and quick release the pressure
13. Serve and enjoy your breakfast!

Nutrition Information

Calories: 151, Fat: 9.2g, Carbohydrates: 16.1g, Dietary Fiber: 0 g, Protein: 1.9g

Recipe 7: Scottish Eggs

TIME TO PREPARE
9 minutes

COOK TIME
15 Minutes

SERVING
4 People

Ingredients

- 4 Eggs
- 1 lb of ground sausage
- 1 Tbsp of vegetable oil
- 1 Pinch of salt
- 1 pinch of black pepper
- ½ Teaspoon of dried mint

Instructions

1. Place the steaming basket in your Instant Pot. Then pour 1 cup of water with the eggs. Close the lid of your Instant Pot and set it at high pressure for around 5 minutes.
2. When the timer beeps, naturally release the pressure for around for 5 minutes, then apply a quick release and turn off the Instant Pot.
3. Cool the eggs into cold water; then remove its shells and split the sausage into pieces of equal size.
4. Season the sausage with the salt, the pepper and the mint and combine it very well with your fingers.
5. Flatten the sausage meat into equal pieces and place your hard boiled eggs right into the centre and then wrap your sausage around it. Repeat it with the rest of the egg halves.
6. Press the button sauté or browning in your Instant Put and add a little bit if oil (No more than 3 tbsp) and sauté your scotch eggs.
7. Once done with sautéing, remove the eggs from the Instant Pot and pour 1 cup of water into it.

8. Place the trivet and line the eggs above the rack or the trivet.
9. Set at high pressure for around 5 minutes and when the timer beeps, quick release the pressure
10. Serve and enjoy the Scotch eggs for your breakfast!

Nutrition Information

Calories: 169, Fat: 8.2g, Carbohydrates: 0.67g, Dietary Fiber: 0.4 g, Protein: 23g

Recipe 8: Instant Pot Breakfast Quiche

TIME TO PREPARE
10 minutes

COOK TIME
30 Minutes

SERVING
6 People

Ingredients

- 6 large and well beaten eggs
- ½ Cup of milk
- ¼ Teaspoon of salt
- 1/8 Teaspoon of ground black pepper
- 4 Slices of bacon and crumbled cooked
- 1 Cup of cooked ground sausage
- ½ Cup of diced ham
- 2 Large chopped green onions
- 1 Cup of shredded cheese

Instructions

1. Start by putting the trivet into the bottom of your Instant Pot; then add 1 and ½ cups of water to it.
2. At the same time and in a separate bowl, place the eggs, the milk, the salt and the pepper; then mix all of the ingredients together and whisk.
3. Add the bacon, the sausage, the ham, the green onions and the cheese until around 1 quart of your soufflé dish is covered.
4. Pour the mixture of the eggs over the top of your meat and stir very well.
5. Cover your soufflé dish and use an aluminum foil to place your pan on the trivet in the Instant Pot.
6. Close the lid and set high pressure for around 30 minutes.
7. When the timer beeps, turn off your Instant Pot and quick release the pressure.
8. Sprinkle cheese and broil the quiche until it becomes golden; then serve and enjoy your breakfast!

Nutrition Information

Calories: 139, Fat: 5g, Carbohydrates: 14g, Dietary Fiber: 0.3 g, Protein: 9g

Recipe 9: Quinoa with Fruits

TIME TO PREPARE
5 minutes

COOK TIME
12 Minutes

SERVING
4 People

Ingredients

- 1 and ½ cups of uncooked and well rinsed quinoa
- 2 and ¼ cups of water
- 2 tbsp of maple syrup
- ½ Teaspoon of vanilla
- ¼ Teaspoon of ground cinnamon
- 1 Pinch of sea salt
- For the topping: you can use milk or fresh berries and sliced almonds

Instructions

1. Add the quinoa with the water, the maple syrup, the vanilla, the cinnamon, and the salt to your Instant Pot.
2. Press the setting high pressure at around 2 minutes
3. When the timer beeps, wait for around 10 minutes and then apply the quick release method and fluff your quinoa.
4. Serve your breakfast hot with the milk, the vanilla, the salt and the cinnamon.
5. Sprinkle with almonds.
6. Enjoy a delicious and nutritious breakfast Quinoa!

Nutrition Information

Calories: 334.9, Fat: 7.3g, Carbohydrates: 59.4g, Dietary Fiber: 6.2 g, Protein: 10.5g

Recipe 10: Potato Frittata

TIME TO PREPARE
9 minutes

COOK TIME
10 Minutes

SERVING
6 People

Ingredients

- 4 oz of raw peeled and thinly sliced Potatoes; soak it in water for 15 minutes before drying it.
- 1 Tbsp of melted Butter
- ¼ Cup of Spanish diced onions.
- ½ Teaspoon of sea Salt
- ¼ Teaspoon of Black Pepper
- 1 Teaspoon of all spice seasoning
- 1 Minced garlic clove
- 2 Tbsp of Baking Mix
- ¼ Cup of Milk
- 1 Teaspoon of Tomato Paste
- 4 Oz of grated Cheese
- 1 and ½ cups of Water

Instructions

1. Start by peeling and slicing the potatoes into very thin strips and soak in water for around 15 minutes.
2. In a deep bowl, whisk all together the eggs with the seasonings until it becomes very well combined.
3. Add the onions and the garlic to the mixture of the eggs. Meanwhile, grease a heat proof dish that fits your Instant Pot.
4. Remove the potatoes from the water and dry it with the use of a paper towel. Then add the raw potatoes and after that pour it into the melted butter.
5. Add the mixture of the eggs and the optional ingredients to top your dish.
6. Sprinkle with the cheese. Meanwhile, pour water into your Instant Pot and place the trivet or the steaming basket in it.
7. Place the baking dish on the trivet of the Instant Pot and lock the lid.
8. Set at high pressure for around 10 minutes.

- For the topping; use: 1 oz of grated cheese and Green Pepper, you can also add Bacon, spinach and ham or sausage

9. When the timer beeps, naturally release the pressure and top with cheese.
10. Serve and enjoy your Frittata!

Nutrition Information

Calories: 260, Fat: 17g, Carbohydrates: 13.8g, Dietary Fiber: 2.4 g, Protein: 15.6g

Recipe 11: Mashed Potatoes with Scrambled Eggs

TIME TO PREPARE
5 minutes

COOK TIME
6 Minutes

SERVING
4 People

Ingredients

- 6 Russet peeled and diced potatoes
- 1 and ½ cups of water
- 4 large beaten eggs
- ¼ Cup of finely chopped onion
- 1 Cup of mayonnaise
- 2 Tbsp of finely chopped and fresh parsley
- 1 Tbsp of dill pickle juice
- 1 Tbsp of mustard
- 1 Pinch of Salt
- 1 pinch of pepper

Instructions

1. Place the steaming basket in your Instant pot and pour the water, the potatoes
2. Add the eggs and close the lid in its place; then set at High Pressure for around 6 minutes.
3. When the timer beeps, turn off your Instant Pot and quick release the pressure, and cool the eggs.
4. Ina deep bowl, combine all together, the mayonnaise, the parsley, the onion and the pickle juice with the mustard; then combine all of the ingredients with the potatoes.
5. Peel your eggs and cut it into dices; then season with salt and pepper.
6. Top with slices of eggs and cheese.
7. Serve and enjoy!

Nutrition Information

Calories: 306, Fat: 14.7g, Carbohydrates: 27.7g, Dietary Fiber: 3.3 g, Protein: 16.5g

Recipe 12: Egg Muffins

TIME TO PREPARE
8 minutes

COOK TIME
20 Minutes

SERVING
8 People

Ingredients

- 5 Large eggs
- ½ Cup of almond or ½ cup of coconut milk
- 1 Cup of finely chopped kale
- ¼ Cup of finely chopped chives
- 1 pinch of salt
- 1 pinch of pepper
- 7 Prosciutto slices

Instructions

1. Pour 1 and ½ cups of water in the Instant Pot and place the trivet inside or the steaming basket.
2. Start by whisking the eggs and add to it your chopped kale; then add the chives.
3. Pour in the coconut milk or almond, the salt, and the pepper. Then mix very well.
4. Grease 8 heat proof muffin cups with your coconut oil and line each of the cups with the use of prosciutto slice.
5. Divide the mixture of your eggs between your muffin cups.
6. Fill the ⅔ of each of the cups
7. Set high pressure for 20 minutes and close the lid of the Instant Pot.
8. Once the timer beeps, quick release the pressure and let the muffins cool a few minutes before serving it.
9. Serve and enjoy your delicious egg muffins!

Nutrition Information

Calories: 166.5, Fat: 11.3g, Carbohydrates: 4.6g, Dietary Fiber: 1.1g, Protein: 11.5g

Recipe 13: Eggs with Mushrooms and Ham

TIME TO PREPARE
4 minutes

COOK TIME
5 Minutes

SERVING
3-4 People

Ingredients

- 3 Large eggs
- 1 Tbsp of water
- ½ Cup of chopped mushrooms
- 1Oz of thinly sliced chopped deli ham
- 2 Tbsp of shredded Swiss cheese
- 1 Pinch of salt
- 1 Pinch of black pepper
- 1 tbsp of finely chopped parsley
- 1 Pinch of cumin
- 1 Teaspoon of ground red pepper

Instructions

1. Start by heating your Instant Pot and pour 1 cup of water in it.
2. Place the trivet inside your Instant Pot.
3. Meanwhile, line three steel or heatproof ramekins and in a separate deep bowl, whisk all together the eggs with the cooking spray.
4. Add the egg, the water, a little bit of red pepper, the mushrooms and the ham.
5. Beat the mixture until it is very – well blended.
6. Add the salt, the parsley, the cumin and the black pepper.
7. Add the cheese and mix very well; then pour the mixture evenly into the ramekins.
8. Top with cheese and line the ramekins in the steaming basket.
9. Set at high pressure for 5 minutes and lock the lid of the Instant Pot.
10. When the timer beeps, quick release the pressure

and serve your breakfast.
11. Enjoy!

Nutrition Information

Calories: 171.3, Fat: 10.4g, Carbohydrates: 4.6g, Dietary Fiber: 1.5g, Protein: 15.5g

CHAPTER 3: RICE AND PASTA RECIPE

Recipe 14: Rice curry with Lamb

TIME TO PREPARE
10 minutes

COOK TIME
15 Minutes

SERVING
4 People

Ingredients

- 1 Tablespoons of vegetable oil
- 1 Medium, peeled and thickly sliced onion
- 1 lb of trimmed of fat and chopped lamb neck fillet
- ½ Teaspoon of ground cumin
- 6 Crushed, cardamom pods with the seeds removed
- ¼ Teaspoon of ground cinnamon
- 1 to 2 bay leaves
- 1 and ½ cups of long-grain white rice
- 1/3 Cup of raisins
- ¾ Cup of dried apricots

Instructions

1. Heat about 2 tablespoons of vegetable oil in your Instant Pot by pressing the button "Sauté"
2. Toss in the onion and cook for about 8 minutes; then remove it and drain it over a paper towel
3. Add the remaining quantity of oil; then brown the meat for about 6 minutes
4. Add the spices and the rice
5. Add in the raising and the apricots and the stock; then close the lid of the Instant Pot; make sure to steak the valve; then set the timer for about 15 minutes and set the pressure to High
6. When the timer beeps; quick release the pressure for 5 minutes; then when it is safe, open the lid
7. Serve the rice curry in bowls and top with chopped parsley; enjoy!

- 2 Cups of vegetable stock
- 2 Tablespoons of fresh parsley leaves

Nutrition Information

Calories: 351| Fat: 10.2g | Carbohydrates: 45.6g | Fiber: 5.8 g |Protein: 20.4g

Recipe 15: Hawaiian-Style Rice with Beef

TIME TO PREPARE
7 minutes

COOK TIME
32 Minutes

SERVING
3-4 People

Ingredients

- 1 Tablespoon of olive oil
- 1 Finely chopped small onion
- 1 Chopped red pepper
- 6 Oz of chopped ham
- 3 Lightly scrambled eggs
- 1 and ½ cups of long-grain white rice, rinsed and drained
- 2 Cups of water
- 2 Tablespoons of soy sauce
- 1 Cup of chopped pineapple
  1 Tablespoon of chopped scallions

Instructions

1. Place the oil, the onion and the red pepper in the bottom of your Instant Pot and press the button "Sauté"
2. Sauté your ingredients for about 3 minutes; then add in the ham and stir your ingredients
3. Add in the beaten eggs and stir again for about 4 minutes
4. Add in the white rice; then pour in the water, the soy sauce and the chopped pineapple; then cover your Instant Pot with the lid and seal the valve; then set the manual timer to about 24 minutes
5. When the timer beeps; quick release the pressure; then let the rice sit in the setting "Keep Warm" for 5 minutes
6. Serve the rice into bowls; then garnish with chopped scallions
7. Serve and enjoy your dish!

Nutrition Information

Calories: 280.1| Fat: 17.8g | Carbohydrates: 17.5g | Fiber: 2.8 g |Protein: 13.4g

Recipe 16: Cajun Rice

TIME TO PREPARE
5 minutes

COOK TIME
12 Minutes

SERVING
4 People

Ingredients

- 2 Tablespoons of oil
- 1 and ½ cups of fresh diced onion
- 1 Cup of diced bell peppers
- ½ Cup of diced celery
- 1 Pound of chopped beef
- 1 Tablespoon of salt-free Cajun seasoning
- 1 Cup of water
- 1 Teaspoon of salt
- 2 Bay leaves
- 1 Teaspoon of dried oregano
- 2 Teaspoons of hot sauce
- 1 Cup of rinsed and drained long-grain white rice

Instructions

1. Turn on your Instant Pot by pressing the button "Sauté" and when it displays hot, add in the oil; then add in the chopped beef and stir for 4 minutes
2. Add in the bay leaf, the Cajun seasoning, the hot sauce, the salt and the rice; then stir for 3 minutes
3. Pour in the broth and lock the lid.
4. Make sure to seal the valve and cook on High pressure for about 5 minutes.
5. When the timer beeps, let the Instant Pot rest for about 10 minutes
6. Release the remaining pressure; then fluff the rice with a fork
7. Serve and enjoy your dish!

Nutrition Information

Calories: 461| Fat: 18g | Carbohydrates: 43g | Fiber: 3 g |Protein: 26g

Recipe 17: Cajun Rice

TIME TO PREPARE
5 minutes

COOK TIME
12 Minutes

SERVING
4 People

Ingredients

- 2 Tablespoons of oil
- 1 and ½ cups of fresh diced onion
- 1 Cup of diced bell peppers
- ½ Cup of diced celery
- 1 Pound of chopped beef
- 1 Tablespoon of salt-free Cajun seasoning
- 1 Cup of water
- 1 Teaspoon of salt
- 2 Bay leaves
- 1 Teaspoon of dried oregano
- 2 Teaspoons of hot sauce
- 1 Cup of rinsed and drained long-grain white rice

Instructions

8. Turn on your Instant Pot by pressing the button "Sauté" and when it displays hot, add in the oil; then add in the chopped beef and stir for 4 minutes
9. Add in the bay leaf, the Cajun seasoning, the hot sauce, the salt and the rice; then stir for 3 minutes
10. Pour in the broth and lock the lid.
11. Make sure to seal the valve and cook on High pressure for about 5 minutes.
12. When the timer beeps, let the Instant Pot rest for about 10 minutes
13. Release the remaining pressure; then fluff the rice with a fork
14. Serve and enjoy your dish!

Nutrition Information

Calories: 461| Fat: 18g | Carbohydrates: 43g | Fiber: 3 g |Protein: 26g

Recipe 18: Jasmine Rice With veggies

TIME TO PREPARE
5 minutes

COOK TIME
5 Minutes

SERVING
5 People

Ingredients

- 2 Cups of Jasmine rice
- 1 Cup of finely chopped carrots
- 1 Can of about 15 ounces of reduced-fat coconut milk
- ½ Cup of water
- 1 Tablespoon of lime juice
- 1 Cup of frozen peas, defrosted
- 1 and ½ tablespoons of rice vinegar

Instructions

1. Place the Jasmine rice in the Instant Pot; then add in the chopped carrots
2. Pour in the water and the coconut milk and lock the lid of your Instant Pot
3. Make sure the valve is in the sealed position; then press the button "Manual/Pressure"
4. Set the timer to about 5 minutes and naturally release the pressure for about 10 minutes
5. Remove the lid when it is safe to do and add in the peas and the lime juice
6. Mix your ingredients very well; then add in the rice vinegar and mix
7. Serve and enjoy your dish!

Nutrition Information

Calories: 310.8| Fat: 5.6g | Carbohydrates: 28g | Fiber: 2.4 g |Protein: 37.5g

Recipe 19: Rice Pilaf with Fennel

TIME TO PREPARE
7 minutes

COOK TIME
40 Minutes

SERVING
4 People

Ingredients

- ¾ Pound of fennel bulb
- ¼ Cup of minced fresh shallots
- 1 and ½ tablespoons of olive oil
- 1 and ½ tablespoons of minced fresh garlic
- 1 Cup of wild rice
- 1 Cup of dry white wine
- 3 Cups of water
- 2 Teaspoons of balsamic vinegar
- ½ Teaspoon of sea salt
- ¼ Teaspoon of freshly ground pepper

Instructions

1. Trim the end of the fennel bulb and discard the end
2. Trim the stalks from the fennel bulb and cut the bulbs in portions; then thinly slice it and set it aside
3. Heat the Instant Pot by pressing the button "Sauté"; then add in 1 tablespoon of oil and sauté the shallots for about 3 minutes
4. Add in the garlic, the fennel and the rice and stir
5. Pour in the wine in 2 and ½ cups of water; then mix very well
6. Lock the lid of the Instant pot and set seal the valve
7. Press the button "multigrain" and the timer to about 35 to 40 minutes
8. When the timer beeps; quick release the pressure; then when it is safe, open the lid of your Instant Pot and fluff the rice with a fork
9. Add in the balsamic vinegar, the salt, and the pepper and press the button sauté; then stir for 5 minutes
10. Serve and enjoy your dish!

Nutrition Information

Calories: 220| Fat: 4g | Carbohydrates: 42g | Fiber: 2 g |Protein: 5g

Recipe 20: Long-Grain Rice with Cranberries

TIME TO PREPARE
6 minutes

COOK TIME
10 Minutes

SERVING
3-4 People

Ingredients

- 1 Cup of long-grain rice
- 2 Cups of water
- 1 Cup of apple juice
- 1 Tablespoon of vegetable oil
- 2 Chopped celery ribs
- 1 Cup of sliced mushrooms
- 3 Chopped scallions
- 1 Cored and chopped apple
- ¼ Cup of dried cranberries
- ¼ Cup of chopped pecan
- ¼ Teaspoon of ground fennel
- ½ Teaspoon of dried sage
- ¼ Teaspoon of ground ginger
- ½ Teaspoon of garlic

Instructions

1. Rinse the rice and drain it very well; then heat the Instant Pot by pressing the button "sauté"
2. Add the rice to your Instant pot; then pour in the water and the apple juice
3. Close the lid of your Instant pot and make sure the valve is in sealed position
4. Set the timer to about 10 minutes and set the pressure to High
5. When the timer beeps, naturally release the pressure and when it is safe, open the Instant Pot and remove the rice from the heat; then drain off any remaining liquid and set aside.
6. Sauté the mushrooms and the celery in 1 tablespoon of oil in a large skillet over a medium high heat for about
7. Add the rice to the skillet and toss your veggies very well
8. Season with 1 pinch of pepper and 1 pinch of salt Serve and enjoy your dish!

        powder
- 1 Pinch of salt
- 1 Pinch of pepper

Nutrition Information

Calories: 222.2| Fat: 8.4g | Carbohydrates: 33.1g | Fiber: 2.2 g |Protein: 4.8g

Recipe 21: Rice with Cilantro and spinach

TIME TO PREPARE
6 minutes

COOK TIME
12 Minutes

SERVING
3-4 People

Ingredients

- ½ Cup of tightly packed fresh cilantro
- 1 Cup of tightly packed fresh spinach leaves
- 1 and ¼ cups of chicken stock
- 1 and ¼ cups of milk
- 1 Teaspoon of salt
- 1 Tablespoon of olive oil
- 3 Tablespoons of unsalted butter
- 1 and ½ cups of long-grain white rice
- ¼ Cup of minced onion
- 1 Minced jalapeno with the seeds removed
- 2 Minced garlic cloves
- 1 Quartered lime

Instructions

1. Add the cilantro, the spinach, the chicken stock, the coconut milk and the salt to a blender and puree until you get a smooth mixture and set it aside
2. Add the olive oil to your Instant Pot and press the button "sauté", and then add in the butter and the onion and sauté for 2 minutes
3. Add the jalapeno and the garlic and sauté for about 1 to 2 minutes; then add the rice and stir
4. Pour in the pureed mixture and mix
5. Lock the lid of your Instant Pot and make sure the valve is in sealed position
6. Set the timer to about 10 minutes and the pressure to High
7. When the timer beeps; quick release the pressure; then turn the valve to venting position
8. Open the lid when it is safe to do
9. Fluff the rice with a fork
10. Serve and enjoy your dish with a squeeze of lemon on top!

Nutrition Information

Calories: 216.6| Fat: 7.8g | Carbohydrates: 31.5g | Fiber: 5.6 g |Protein: 8.5g

Recipe 22: Rice with Cashews

TIME TO PREPARE
6 minutes

COOK TIME
14 Minutes

SERVING
3-4 People

Ingredients

- 1 Tablespoon of olive oil
- 2 Finely minced garlic cloves
- 1 Cup of rinsed and de-seeded salted olives
- 1 Dash of pepper
- 1 and ½ cups of long-grain white rice, rinsed and drained
- 1 Cup of basmati rice
- 1 Diced red chilli
- 2 Tablespoons of chopped cashews
- 1 Tablespoon of sesame oil

Instructions

1. Heat your Instant Pot by pressing the button "Sauté"
2. Add the oil to the Instant Pot; then add in the garlic and sauté for a couple of minutes
3. Add in the olives, the pepper and the rinsed rice
4. Add the sesame oil and toss again; then pour in 1 and ¼ cups of water
5. Close the Instant Pot and seal the valve
6. Set the timer to about 12 minutes on a High Pressure
7. When the timer beeps; naturally release the pressure for about 10 minutes
8. Turn the valve to the vent position and open the lid
9. Fluff the rice with a fork; then sprinkle the chilli, the cashews and the sesame oil and mix
10. Serve and enjoy your dish!

Nutrition Information

Calories: 366.6| Fat: 16.3g | Carbohydrates: 43.9g | Fiber: 1.2 g |Protein: 11.2g

Recipe 23: Rice with Avocado

TIME TO PREPARE
5 minutes

COOK TIME
10 Minutes

SERVING
3 People

Ingredients

- 2 and ¼ cups of water
- 1 Tablespoon of butter
- 2 Teaspoons of reduced-sodium chicken stock
- ¾ Teaspoon of ground cumin
- 1 Cup of uncooked long-grain white rice
- 1/3 Cup of picante sauce
- 1 Medium, peeled and cubed ripe avocado
- 2 Sliced green onions

Instructions

1. Heat your Instant Pot by pressing the button "sauté"; then pour in the water, the rice and the salt and close the lid of your Instant Pot and seal the valve
2. Set the timer to about 10 minutes and the pressure to High
3. When the timer beeps, naturally release the pressure for about 10 minutes
4. Open the lid of the Instant Pot and add in the picante sauce and stir
5. Add in the avocado and the green onions and mix
6. Serve and enjoy your delicious rice!

Nutrition Information

Calories: 239.2 | Fat: 14.9g | Carbohydrates: 21.4g | Fiber: 4.1 g | Protein: 7g

RECIPE 24: RICE WITH LENTILS AND PEAS

TIME TO PREPARE
5 minutes

COOK TIME
6 Minutes

SERVING
4-5 People

Ingredients

- 1 Cup of long-grain white rice, soaked in water for about 10 minutes
- 2 Tablespoons of coconut oil
- 2 Tablespoons of coconut oil
- 1 Teaspoon of black mustard seeds
- 1 Tablespoon of split chickpeas
- 1 Tablespoon of split and skinless black lentil
- 14 Curry leaves
- 1 and ½ cups of cashews, split into halves
- 1 Green chilli
- 2 Cups of frozen, grated coconut
- 1 and ½ cups of water
- 1 Teaspoon of salt

Instructions

1. Soak the white rice in cold water for about 15 minutes
2. Rinse the rice and drain it; then set it aside
3. Press the 'sauté' button on your Instant Pot; then add in the coconut oil and once it melts, add in the mustard seeds; then split the chickpeas and the skinless black lentils
4. Once the mustard seeds start popping up; add in the curry leaves, the cashews and the pepper and stir for about 30 seconds
5. Add in the grated coconut and stir for about 30 additional seconds
6. Add in the rice and pour in the water and season with the salt and mix
7. Secure the lid of your Instant Pot and seal the valve; then set the timer to about 6 minutes at a High pressure
8. When the timer beeps; then turn naturally release the pressure for about 10 minutes
9. Open the valve and release the remaining pressure
10. Fluff the rice with a fork; then serve and enjoy its delicious taste!

Nutrition Information

Calories: 104.1| Fat: 1.7g | Carbohydrates: 13.7g | Fiber: 3g |Protein: 8.7g

Recipe 25: Spicy White Rice with Chili and Cumin

TIME TO PREPARE
5 minutes

COOK TIME
6 Minutes

SERVING
4 People

Ingredients

- 1 ½ tablespoons of olive oil
- ½ cup of finely chopped sweet onion
- 1 Finely minced garlic clove
- 1 ½ cups of vegetable broth
- ¼ Cup of tomato sauce
- 1 Pinch of Chili powder
- ½ Teaspoon of cumin
- ½ Teaspoon of salt
- 1 Pinch of pepper
- 1 cup of white rice

Instructions

1. Heat your Instant Pot by pressing the "sauté" function on your Instant Pot and heat the oil
2. Add in the onion and sauté the mixture for about 3 minutes
3. Add in the garlic and sauté for about 2 additional minutes
4. Close the lid of your Instant Pot and seal the valve; then press the button "manual" and set the timer for about 6 minutes at a High Pressure
5. When the timer beeps; quick release the pressure; then naturally release the pressure for 10 minutes
6. Carefully open the lid of the Instant Pot and fluff the rice with a fork
7. Serve and enjoy your delicious dish!

Nutrition Information

Calories: 223| Fat: 4.5g | Carbohydrates: 39.8g | Fiber: 0g |Protein: 4.8g

Recipe 26: Rice with Black Beans

TIME TO PREPARE
7 minutes

COOK TIME
20 Minutes

SERVING
5 People

Ingredients

- 2 Cups of canned, drained and rinsed black beans
- 2 Finely minced garlic cloves
- 1 Finely chopped large red bell pepper
- ½ Large finely chopped red onion
- 2 Cups of frozen corn
- 2 Cups of brown rice, rinsed and drained
- 1 Juiced lime
- 1 Tablespoon of Chili powder
- 1 Tablespoon of paprika
- 1 Tablespoon of cumin
- ½ Teaspoon of salt
- ¼ Teaspoon of ground black pepper
- 1 Tablespoon of oil

Instructions

1. In your Instant Pot, add in the oil, the onions and the peppers and press the button "sauté"
2. Sauté your ingredients for about 5 minutes; then add in the garlic and sauté for about 3 minutes
3. Add in the chilli powder, the paprika, the cumin, the salt, and the black pepper and stir for about 3 minutes
4. Add in the black beans and the brown rice and pour in 1 cups of vegetable stock
5. Close the lid of the Instant Pot and make sure the valve is sealed
6. Set the timer for about 20 minutes at High pressure
7. When the timer beeps; quick release the pressure for about 10 minutes
8. Turn the valve to venting position and release any remaining pressure
9. Open the lid of the Instant Pot and add in the corn, the lime and the juice
10. Fluff the rice with a fork; then serve and enjoy your dish with chopped avocado!

- ½ Chopped Avocado
½ Cup of light sour cream

Nutrition Information

Calories: 152.9| Fat: 1.8g | Carbohydrates: 26.1g | Fiber: 8.5g |Protein: 8.5g

RECIPE 27: SWEET POTATO COCONUT RICE

TIME TO PREPARE
5 minutes

COOK TIME
12 Minutes

SERVING
3 People

Ingredients

- 1 Sweet; large, cooked, peeled and cubed potato
- 2 Cups of long-grain white rice
- 3 Cups of vegetable broth
- 3 Cups of water
- ½ Teaspoon of salt
- 1 Teaspoon of garlic powder
- 1 and ½ teaspoons of ginger powder
- ⅛ Teaspoons of cayenne
- ¼ Teaspoon of pepper
- 2 Bay leaves
- 1 Large, finely chopped sweet onion
- ½ Cup of maple syrup
- ½ Cup of full-fat coconut milk
- ½ Cup of golden or

Instructions

1. Heat your Instant by pressing the button "Sauté"
2. Add in the rice, the water, the veggie broth, the salt, the spices and the bay leaves
3. Close the lid of your Instant pot and make sure the lid is in sealed position
4. Set the timer to about 12 minutes at High pressure
5. When the timer beeps; quick release the pressure for about 10 minutes
6. Open the lid of the Instant pot when it is safe to do it
7. Stir in the coconut milk, the raisins, the shredded coconut, and the cashews, if using and mix with a spoon
8. Add in the cubed sweet potatoes and gently mix again
9. Serve and enjoy your dish!

black raisins
- 1 Cup of shredded unsweetened coconut
- 1 Cup of cashews

Nutrition Information

Calories: 396| Fat: 9g | Carbohydrates: 54g | Fiber: 7g |Protein: 12g

Recipe 28: Shrimp Scampi

TIME TO PREPARE
6 minutes

COOK TIME
9 Minutes

SERVING
3-4 People

Ingredients

- 2 Tablespoons of butter
- 1 tbsp of olive oil
- 3 minced garlic cloves garlic
- 2 whole minced shallots
- 1/4 Cup of white wine
- 2 lb of peeled shrimp
- 12 oz of angel hair pasta, broken into half
- 3 cups of chicken stock
- 1/2 whole fresh lemon
- 1 pinch of sea salt and 1 pinch of pepper, to taste
- 1/4 tsp of red pepper flakes
- 1 tbsp of fresh parsley
- 2 tbsp of capers

Instructions

1. Turn on your instant pot on the sauté mode; then melt the butter; and add the oil, the garlic and the shallots.
2. Sauté for about 2 to 3 minutes; then add the wine and cook for about 3 minutes
3. Add the shrimp; then season with 1 pinch of salt, 1 pinch of pepper and pepper flakes.
4. Sprinkle with the fresh lemon and sauté for about 3 additional minutes
5. Remove the shrimp from the Instant Pot; then add in the chicken stock and the pasta
6. Separate the pasta; then top woth the shrimp and cover your pot
7. Cancel the sauté mode and turn your Instant Pot on High for about 3 minutes
8. When the time is up; quickly release all the pressure; then open the instant pot and add the capers
9. Stir your ingredients; then season with fresh parsley
10. Top with the fresh Parmigiana cheese.
11. Serve and enjoy your Shrimp Scampi!

Nutrition Information

Calories: 358.3 | Fat: 19.8g | Carbohydrates: 5.4g | Fiber: 0.5g | Protein: 37.4g

Recipe 29: Bruschetta Chicken Pasta

TIME TO PREPARE
5 minutes

COOK TIME
3 Minutes

SERVING
3 People

Ingredients

- 1 tbsp of olive oil
- 2 medium-sized boneless and skinless chopped chicken breasts into pieces of about 1 inch each
- 2 Minced Garlic cloves garlic
- 4 Cups of water
- 1 lb of rotini pasta
- 1 Jar of about 280 mL of jarred roasted

Instructions

1. Add the olive oil, the chicken, the garlic, the water and the Rotini pasta to the Instant Pot
2. Cook on a high pressure for about 3 minutes; then apply a quick pressure release; the instant Pot will take approximately 10 to 15 minutes to preheat
3. In the meantime; chop the jarred tomatoes; then make the Bruschetta by mixing all its ingredients together.
4. Open the lid to the Instant Pot when it is safe to do so and when all the pressure has been released.
5. Stir in the cherry tomatoes, the parmesan cheese

- cherry tomatoes
  - 1 Cup of grated parmesan cheese

For the BRUSCHETTA

- 5 Chopped plum tomatoes
- 1 Chopped small red onion
- 2 tbsp of olive oil
- 2 Minced garlic cloves
- 1/2 Cup of chopped fresh basil
- 1/2 tsp of Salt
- 1/2 tsp of pepper

and the Bruschetta and mix very well
6. Garnish with some extra chopped fresh basil
7. Serve and enjoy your dish!

Nutrition Information

Calories: 378| Fat: 9.2g | Carbohydrates: 50.4g | Fiber: 5.8g |Protein: 21.3g

CHAPTER 4: VEGETABLES, GRAINS AND BEANS RECIPES

Recipe 30: Vegetables Medley Instant Pot

TIME TO PREPARE
4 minutes

COOK TIME
5 Minutes

SERVING
3 People

Ingredients

- A bag of 2 pounds of fresh broccoli, carrots, cauliflower, all prewashed
- 8 ounces of whipped cream cheese
- 1/4 cup of milk
- The zest of 1 lemon
- The juice of 1/2 lemon
- 1/4 teaspoon of garlic powder
- 1/4 teaspoon of oregano
- 1/4 teaspoon of dried parsley
- 1/4 teaspoon of dried basil
- 1/4 teaspoon of salt
- 1/8 teaspoon of onion powder
- 1 pinch of black pepper
- 1 pinch of thyme

Instructions

1. Add about 1 cup of water to your Electric pressure cooker pot.
2. Place the carrots into water; then place a steamer basket on top of the carrots
3. Add the broccoli and the cauliflower
4. Secure the lid and turn the pressure release knob to a sealed position
5. Cook at a High pressure for about 1 minute
6. When the cooking process is complete; use a quick release method
7. While holding the handle, remove the collapsible steamer basket from your Instant Pot.
8. Drain the water from the carrots; then add the carrots to the basket and set it aside
9. Return the ingredients to the pressure cooker; then add in the cream mixture and select the button sauté
10. Stir and select the sauté button and let the cheese melt; then add in the vegetables to the Instant Pot
11. Gently stir; then add a splash of lemon and salt
12. Serve and enjoy your dish!

Nutrition Information

Calories: 98 | Fat: 4.1g | Carbohydrates: 12.3g | Fiber: 3.3g | Protein: 4.7g

Recipe 31: Instant Pot Pinto Beans

TIME TO PREPARE
10 minutes

COOK TIME
35 Minutes

SERVING
4 People

Ingredients

- 1 Tbsp of cooking oil
- 4 Oz of dry chorizo
- 1 Medium yellow onion
- 3 Garlic cloves
- 2 Cups of dry pinto beans
- 2 to 3 bay leaves
- 1 Pinch of freshly cracked pepper
- 3 cups of reduced sodium chicken broth
- 1 Can of 15 oz of diced tomatoes

Instructions

1. Chop the chorizo; then add it to your Instant Pot together with the oil
2. Press the button sauté; then adjust to the select the temperature button "less" setting
3. Sauté the chorizo into the oil with the lid until it becomes slightly crispy
4. While the chorizo is sautéing; chop the onion and mince the garlic
5. Once the chorizo becomes crispy; add in the onion and the garlic and continue to sauté until the onion becomes soft and transparent
6. Add in the beans, the bay leaves, and the pepper to the Instant Pot
7. Add in the broth; and stir; then cover the Instant Pot with a lid
8. Close the steam valve; then press the manual button and select High pressure and press the button + to increase the time to about 35 minutes
9. Let the beans cook for about 35 minutes; then let the pressure naturally release
10. Add in the canned chopped tomatoes with all the juices and stir

11. Press the cancel button "Keep warm" function; then press the button sauté and use the adjust button to select the "normal" heat level
12. Let the mixture slowly simmer and stir very often until the liquid thickens up.
13. Serve the beans with the tortillas, the tortilla chips, or over rice with grated cheese, chopped cilantro and finely diced red onion.

Nutrition Information

Calories: 245| Fat: 1g | Carbohydrates: 45g | Fiber: 15g |Protein: 15g

Recipe 32: Lentil Spicy Gumbo

TIME TO PREPARE
7 minutes

COOK TIME
15 Minutes

SERVING
3-4 People

Ingredients

- 1 tbsp of olive oil
- 1 tsp of minced garlic or 2 cloves
- 1 Finely chopped red bell Pepper
- 1 1/2 finely chopped onion
- 2 celery ribs
- 1 tbsp of fresh thyme or 1 tsp dried
- 1/2 tbsp of fresh oregano
- 1/2 to 1 tsp of Cajun mix spice
- 1/2 tsp of cayenne
- 1 Cup of lentils
- 3 Cups of vegetable broth
- 2 Cups of fresh or frozen chopped okra
- 1 Can of salt free diced tomatoes
- 2 tbsp of Apple Cider Vinegar

Instructions

1. Sauté the oil, the onion, the garlic, the bell pepper, and the celery for about 5 minutes on the sauté setting
2. Add the spices and mix again for about 1 additional minute.
3. Add the remaining ingredients; except for the salt and the pepper and mix very well together
4. Place the lid over your electric pressure cooker; then place the setting on pressure cook at High for about 12 minutes; here the natural release will work much better; but it is best to make sure that the lentils are perfectly cooked
5. After the cooking process ends; add in 1/2 tsp of sea salt or of kosher salt.
6. Season with 1 pinch of black Pepper
7. Stir in the cornstarch; and keep warm for about 10 additional minutes.
8. Don't add any extra salt to the lentil gumbo while pressure cooking
9. Garnish with chopped red pepper flakes
10. Serve and enjoy over rice!

- 1/2 cup of tomato sauce, salt free
- 1 Cup of finely chopped or riced cauliflower
- 1 Pinch of Kosher Salt or sea salt and pepper to taste
- 1 Sliced jalapeño
- Chopped fresh cilantro to garnish
- 1 to 2 tablespoons of tapioca starch

Nutrition Information

Calories: 230| Fat: 1g | Carbohydrates: 38g | Fiber: 8g |Protein: 15g

Recipe 33: Instant Pot Red beans

TIME TO PREPARE
7 minutes

COOK TIME
15 Minutes

SERVING
4 People

Ingredients

- 1/2 lb of smoked sausage
- 1 Tbsp of olive oil
- 1 Medium onion
- 1 Chopped bell pepper
- 3 Celery Stalks
- 4 Garlic cloves
- 1 lb of dry uncooked red beans
- 1 tsp of dried thyme
- 1 tsp of dried oregano
- 1 tsp of smoked paprika
- 1/4 tsp of cayenne
- 1 Pinch of freshly cracked black pepper
- 3 cups of chicken broth
- 2 cups of water
- 3 Sliced green onions
- 6 Cups of cooked rice

Instructions

1. Start by slicing the smoked sausage into medallions
2. Add the olive oil and the sliced sausage to your Instant Pot and sauté the sausage for about 5 minutes
3. Remove the sausage from the Instant Pot with a slotted spoon
4. Finely chop the onion, the bell pepper, and the celery; then mince the garlic
5. After removing the sausage of the Instant Pot; add in the onion, the bell pepper, the celery and the garlic and too the Instant Pot and sauté for 5 additional minutes
6. Rinse the beans; then add it to the Instant pot with the sausage, the thyme, the oregano, the paprika, the cayenne and some of the freshly cracked pepper
7. Add in the chicken broth and the water and stir very well to combine
8. Secure the lid on your Instant Pot; then close the vent and close the vent
9. Cook on a High Pressure for about 35 minutes by using the manual button or the bean/chili button
10. When the cooking cycle is over, let the pressure

naturally release
11. Once the beans are very soft; season with salt to your taste
12. Top with 1 cup of rice and sprinkle with sliced green onions
13. Serve and enjoy your dish!

Nutrition Information

Calories: 225| Fat: 0.9g | Carbohydrates: 40.4g | Fiber: 8g |Protein: 15.3g

Recipe 34: Instant Pot Spicy Chickpeas with Cumin

TIME TO PREPARE
10 minutes

COOK TIME
20 Minutes

SERVING
3 People

Ingredients

- 2 Cups of Chickpeas
- 1 Cup of dry Cannellini beans
- ½ Cup of perlated Barley
- 1 Finely minced garlic cloves
- 1 Tbsp of olive Oil
- 1 Pinch of black pepper.
- 3 Coriander seeds
- 4 cups of water
- 2 Teaspoons of salt
- 2 Tbsp of Extra Virgin Olive Oil
- 2 Tbsp of Ricotta

Instructions

1. Soak the chick peas and the beans in two separate bowls overnight before cooking the chickpeas bowl.
2. Rinse the quantity of chickpeas you have and place it in the Instant Pot together with the minced garlic clove and add the spices, the water, the barley and the salt.
3. Add around 1 tbsp of Oil and pour the beans into the steaming basket and place it above the chickpeas.
4. Close and tightly lock the lid of your Instant Pot.
5. Set the heat to high and high pressure for 20 minutes.
6. Once the timer beeps, naturally release the pressure for 15 minutes and pour the beans on the chickpeas.
7. Adjust the taste of salt and pepper.
8. Add 1 teaspoon of cumin and stir very well; then serve and enjoy your chickpeas with ketchup and drizzle olive oil.
9. Enjoy!

Nutrition Information

Calories: 269| Fat: 4g | Carbohydrates: 45g | Fiber: 6g |Protein: 15g

RECIPE 35: SPICY QUINOA CHILI

TIME TO PREPARE
6 minutes

COOK TIME
15 Minutes

SERVING
3-4 People

Ingredients

- 6 Poblano peppers
- 1 Cup of chopped onion
- ½ Cup of chopped red pepper
- 2 teaspoons of minced garlic
- ½ Cup of thawed frozen corn
- 1 Cup of cooked quinoa
- 1 Teaspoon of smoked paprika
- 1 Teaspoon of ground cumin
- ¼ Cup of chopped cilantro
- ½ Cup of fine corn flour
- 1 Cup of unsweetened almond milk
- 1 cup of chopped onion
- 1 teaspoon of minced garlic
- 1 teaspoon of sea salt

Instructions

1. Pour 2 tbsp of olive oil in your Instant Pot and heat it.
2. Sauté the onion and the red pepper for 6 minutes
3. Add the garlic, the corn, the quinoa and the cumin and cook for 3 more minutes.
4. Add the cilantro and the pepper; then cook for 2 more minutes.
5. Add the rest of the ingredients and pour ½ cup of water; then close the lid of the Instant Pot and set at high pressure for 15 minutes.
6. When the timer beeps, quick release the pressure.
7. Serve and enjoy your quinoa!

- ½ teaspoon of fresh ground pepper

Nutrition Information

Calories: 208.4| Fat: 4.2g | Carbohydrates: 34.3g | Fiber: 7g |Protein: 9.3g

Recipe 36: Cauliflower Curry

TIME TO PREPARE
5 minutes

COOK TIME
25 Minutes

SERVING
3 People

Ingredients

- 1 Tbsp of vegetable oil
- 1 Sliced brown onion
- 2 Crushed garlic cloves
- ½ Small and finely grated ginger
- 1 Tbsp of madras curry powder
- 1 lb of crushed tomatoes
- 2 Cups of vegetable stock
- 1lb of peeled and coarsely chopped potatoes
- ½ Small trimmed and cut head cauliflower into florets
- 1 Cup of frozen peas
- 1 Cup of baby spinach leaves
- Steamed rice for

Instructions

1. Heat the oil in your Instant Pot over a medium heat and add the onion.
2. Press the button sauté and cook the onion for around 7 minutes.
3. Add the ginger, the garlic and the curry powder. Cook for 3 more minutes.
4. Add the stock, the tomato, the potato and the cauliflower and press boil.
5. Close the lid of the Instant Pot and set at high pressure for 15 minutes.
6. When the timer beeps, quick release the pressure; then add the baby spinach and the peas and cook for 5 more minutes with the lid open.
7. Serve your nutritious and delicious vegetable curry with rice and with mango chutney.

serving
- Mango chutney (Optional)

Nutrition Information

Calories: 116.1| Fat: 1g | Carbohydrates: 25.2g | Fiber: 9.8g |Protein: 6.5g

Recipe 37: Pumpkin Curry

TIME TO PREPARE
5 minutes

COOK TIME
15 Minutes

SERVING
4-5 People

Ingredients

- 2 Tbsp of vegetable oil
- ½ Teaspoon of cumin seeds
- 1 Cinnamon stick
- 1 Small and finely chopped brown onion
- 5 Minced garlic cloves
- 1 Finely chopped red bird's eye chilli
- ½ Teaspoon of ground coriander
- 1lb of Kent peeled and diced pumpkin

Instructions

1. Heat the oil in your Instant Pot over a medium heat.
2. Add the cinnamon and the cumin.
3. Add the onion and press the button "Sauté" for around 5 minutes.
4. Add the garlic, the chili and the coriander and cook for 2 more minutes.
5. Add the pumpkin, the salt and the pepper; then stir and add 1 cup of water.
6. Close the lid of the Instant Pot and set high pressure for around 15 minutes.
7. When the timer beeps, quick release the pressure and serve your curry with garnishing of your choice.

Nutrition Information

Calories: 191| Fat: 11g | Carbohydrates: 21g | Fiber: 3.7g |Protein: 5.3g

Recipe 38: Veggie Falafel

TIME TO PREPARE
5 minutes

COOK TIME
8 Minutes

SERVING
7 People

Ingredients

- 1 and ½ cups of dry chickpeas
- ½ Cup of chopped fresh parsley
- ½ Cup of chopped white onion
- 6 Minced garlic cloves
- 2 Tbsp of oat flour
- 1 and ½ teaspoon of sea salt
- 1 Tbsp of ground cumin
- 1 Pinch of ground cardamom
- 1 Teaspoon of ground coriander
- 1 Pinch of cayenne pepper

Instructions

1. Start by rinsing the soaking the chickpeas overnight. Once you are ready to cook, place the chickpeas in your Instant Pot.
2. Pour 2 and ½ cups of water in your Instant Pot and close the lid. Set at high pressure for 20 minutes.
3. Meanwhile, combine the parsley, the onion and the garlic all into a food processor.
4. Once the timer beeps drain the chickpeas and add it to the food processor.
5. Add the oat flour, the salt, the cumin, the cardamom, the coriander and the cayenne. Mix very well for 5 minutes.
6. Cover the chickpeas for around 1 hour in the refrigerator. Once it is cooled, remove the mixture from the refrigerator and take out of the mixture around ½ Tbsp of the mixture and make tiny discs with your hands.
7. If you notice the falafel is sticky, sprinkle with a little bit of flour over it or dust it with bread crumbs. Once you finished forming your falafel, line your falafel into a greased baking dish that fits your Steaming basket.
8. Make sure you have poured 1 cup of water in the Instant pot.

9. Close the lid of the Instant Pot and set at high pressure for 5 minutes.
10. Once the timer beeps, quick release the pressure and flip the falafel on the other side and cook for 3 more minutes!

Nutrition Information

Calories: 160| Fat: 7g | Carbohydrates: 18g | Fiber: 3.7g |Protein: 5g

Recipe 39: Stuffed Peppers

TIME TO PREPARE
10 minutes

COOK TIME
25 Minutes

SERVING
6 People

Ingredients

- 2 eggs
- 5 Tbsp of parsley
- ½ cup of cornstarch or ground bread
- ½ Cup of uncooked long grain rice (White)
- 1 Cup of water
- 6 Bell peppers, green or red to your taste
- Tomato sauce
- 1 Tbsp of Worcestershire sauce
- ¼ Teaspoon of garlic powder
- ¼ Teaspoon of onion powder
- 1 pinch of salt
- 1 pinch of pepper
- 1 Teaspoon of Italian seasoning

Instructions

1. Pour 1 and ½ cup of water into your Instant Pot and press boil; then add the rice and reduce the heat.
2. Let the rice simmer for 20 minutes.
3. Clean the pepper and then remove the tops, the seeds, and the membranes of your bell peppers.
4. Arrange your peppers into a baking tray that fits your Instant or
5. In a deep bowl, mix the cooked rice, the parsley, ½ tbsp of tomato sauce, the Worcestershire sauce, the garlic powder, the onion powder, the salt, and the pepper; then add the bread crumbs.
6. Spoon your mixture into the hollowed peppers.
7. Line your stuffed pepper in the dish and slide the dish in the steaming basket of the Instant Pot.
8. Cover the lid of the Instant Pot and set at high pressure for around 25 minutes.
9. When the timer beeps, quick release the pressure, then serve and enjoy your nutritious and healthy stuffed peppers!

Nutrition Information

Calories: 210| Fat: 3g | Carbohydrates: 23g | Fiber: 4.1g |Protein: 10g

Recipe 40: Stuffed Mushrooms

TIME TO PREPARE
6 minutes

COOK TIME
10 Minutes

SERVING
7-8 People

Ingredients

- 15 Button mushrooms

FOR THE STUFFING of the mushrooms

- 1 and ½ slices of bread
- 1 Crushed garlic clove
- 3 Tbsp of finely chopped fresh parsley
- 1 pinch of ground black pepper
- 1 and ½ tbsp of olive oil
- ½ Cup of grated cheese

Instructions

1. In a food processor, grind all together the bread into very fine crumbs and then combine it with the garlic, the parsley and the pepper.
2. When the ingredients are very well mixed, pour in the olive oil.
3. Cut the stalks of the mushrooms and stuff the caps with the ready bread crumbs.
4. Pat the bread crumbs into the caps very well so that you will assure no crumbs will get spilled in the Instant Pot.
5. Meanwhile, prepare your Instant Pot by pouring 1 cup of salt into the bottom of the Instant Pot to make an environment similar to that of oven.
6. Grease a pan baking dish that fits your Instant Pot.
7. Sprinkle the cheese over the mushrooms and line it in the baking tray; then place it in the Instant Pot.
8. Set at high pressure for around 10 minutes.
9. When the timer beeps, quick release the pressure and serve your mushrooms

Nutrition Information

Calories: 78.6| Fat: 4.5g | Carbohydrates: 5.6g | Fiber: 2.3g |Protein: 5.9g

Recipe 41: Stuffed Cabbage

TIME TO PREPARE
15 minutes

COOK TIME
30 Minutes

SERVING
8 People

Ingredients

- 12 leaves of cabbage
- 1 Cup of cooked white rice
- 1 beaten egg
- ¼ Cup of milk
- ¼ Cup of minced onion
- 1 lb of ground beef
- 1 and ¼ teaspoons of salt
- 1 and ¼ teaspoons of ground black pepper
- 1 Can of tomato sauce
- 1 Tbsp of brown sugar
- 1 Tbsp of lemon juice
- 1 Teaspoon of Worcestershire sauce

Instructions

1. Start by removing the cores of the cabbage and place the entire head of cabbage above the trivet of the Instant Pot.
2. Place the whole head of cabbage on a trivet in your Instant Pot with one cup of water. Close the lid of the Instant Pot and set at high pressure for around 15 minutes
3. Once the timer beeps, quick release the pressure and drain the Instant Pot; set the cabbage aside and place the rice in your Instant Pot.
4. Add 2 and ½ cups of water; add the chopped onion, the beef and the cubed tomatoes; then cook for 10 minutes at high pressure.
5. When the timer beeps, quick release the pressure and make sure you have obtained a thick mixture. Line your cabbage above a flat service and tuck the mixture of rice inside it.
6. Roll up the cabbage above the rice. Pour half of your tomato can into the Instant Pot and add 1 cup of water
7. Combine the tomato with the water and line your cabbage rolls inside the Instant Pot.

8. Close the lid of the Instant Pot and set at high pressure for 15 minutes.
9. Once the timer beeps, quick release the pressure.
10. Serve and enjoy a nutritious and stuffed cabbage!

Nutrition Information

Calories: 173.7| Fat: 10.3g | Carbohydrates: 10.4g | Fiber: 2.2g |Protein: 9.8g

Recipe 42: Instant Pot Hummus

TIME TO PREPARE
5 minutes

COOK TIME
10 Minutes

SERVING
4 People

Ingredients

- 1 Can of drained garbanzo beans
- 1 Tbsp of lemon juice
- 1 Tbsp of olive oil
- 1 Minced garlic clove
- ½ Teaspoon of ground cumin
- ½ Teaspoon of salt
- 2 Drops of sesame oil

Instructions

1. Place your Instant Pot over a medium heat and pour 1 and ½ cups of water inside it
2. Add the beans to the Instant Pot and close the lid; then set at high pressure for around 10 minutes
3. Once the timer beeps, quick release the pressure; then remove the beans and blend it with a food processor.
4. Transfer the beans to a deep bowl; add the olive oil, the lemon juice, the garlic, the cumin the salt and the sesame oil and mix very well.
5. Serve and enjoy your delicious hummus!

Nutrition Information

Calories: 65.2| Fat: 1.8g | Carbohydrates: 11.2g | Fiber: 2.9g |Protein: 3.6g

CHAPTER 5: SOUPS AND STEWS RECIPES

Recipe 43: Butternut squash soup

TIME TO PREPARE
5 minutes

COOK TIME
10 Minutes

SERVING
4 People

Ingredients

- 1 Peeled and diced Butternut squash.
- 1 Peeled and diced apple
- 1 Tbsp of Ginger powder or you can use pureed ginger
- 4 Cups of chicken broth
- 2 Tbsp of Coconut oil to taste

Instructions

1. Start by hitting the sauté button on the Instant you are using so that you pre-heat it.
2. When you become able to see the word "HOT", add the coconuts oil and add some of the butternut squash cubes to it then brown it ever lightly for approximately 5 minutes. Now, add the remaining quantity of squash and also add the rest of your ingredients.
3. Close; then lock your Instant Pot.
4. Now, press your manual and use the + for you to add 10 more minutes at high pressure to the cooking time.
5. When the time is over, open the instant pot by using the Quick Release.
6. Puree your mixture by using a blender right in your instant pot or you can also take the mixture out of the instant pot and place it into a blender.
7. Serve and enjoy your delicious and healthy soup.

Nutrition Information

Calories: 110| Fat: 2.5g | Carbohydrates: 22g | Fiber: 2g |Protein: 2g

Recipe 44: Chicken Soup

TIME TO PREPARE
6 minutes

COOK TIME
20 Minutes

SERVING
4 People

Ingredients

- 3 lb of pastured chicken
- 2 roughly chopped carrots
- 1 roughly chopped celery stalk
- ½ radish or turnip chopped into small cubes
- 1 Tbsp of dried parsley
- 1Tbsp of thyme
- 1Tbsp of thyme and rosemary
- 1Tbsp of rosemary
- 2 bay leaves
- 3 crushed garlic cloves
- 1 Medium sliced red or white onion
- 1 Tbsp of sea salt
- 1 teaspoon of freshly ground black pepper
- 1 Finely chopped scallion or chopped green onion

Instructions

1. In the liner of your Instant Pot, place the vegetables; then add the chicken and then add the herbs on the top.
2. Add around 4 to Cups of water.
3. Tightly close the lid and then close the vent.
4. Press the setting of SOUP
5. When the timer beeps, naturally release the pressure for around 20 minutes.
6. Open the lid of the Instant Pot, remove the chicken and debone it; then reserve it to prepare the broth
7. Place the meat back into the Instant Pot
8. Smash the carrots and the celery against the side of the pot
9. Add 1 pinch of salt and 1 pinch pepper according to the taste.
10. Garnish the soup with the sliced onion and the scallion
11. Ladle the soup into bowls
12. Serve and enjoy your soup!

Nutrition Information

Calories: 90| Fat: 2g | Carbohydrates: 6g | Fiber: 1g |Protein: 11g

Recipe 45: Chicken Curry Soup

TIME TO PREPARE
7 minutes

COOK TIME
25 Minutes

SERVING
3-4 People

Ingredients

- 1 and ½ bone-in chicken halved breast
- 3 Diagonally sliced medium carrots
- 2 bay leaves
- 1 Pinch of Kosher salt
- 6 cups of low-sodium chicken broth
- 2 tablespoons of unsalted butter
- 1 thinly sliced large onion
- 1 teaspoon of sugar
- 1 and ½ teaspoons of Madras curry powder
- 1/3 Cup of jasmine rice
- 3 tablespoons of finely chopped fresh mint
- 3 tablespoons of chopped fresh dill

Instructions

1. Combine your chicken, the carrots, the bay leaf and 1 pinch of salt into your Instant Pot.
2. Add around 3 cups of broth and press boil at a medium heat.
3. Close the lid of the instant Pot and set at high pressure to around 10 to 15 minutes.
4. In the meantime; heat the quantity of butter over a medium low heat in a deep sauce pan.
5. Add the sugar and the onion with 1 pinch of salt and cook for around 5 minutes
6. Add the powder of curry and cook for around 2 minutes
7. When the timer beeps, add the broth and the rice; then set the heat to high and let simmer for 10 minutes
8. Take the chicken out of the broth and shred the chicken meat into small pieces; then place it back in the broth.
9. Puree the mixture of the rice with a blender until it becomes smooth and then pour it into the mixture of the shredded chicken and the broth and let simmer for around 5 minutes

- 1 lemon sliced into thin wedges

10. Once the soup is ready, garnish with herbs and then serve it with lemon
11. Enjoy!

Nutrition Information

Calories: 147.2| Fat: 5.1g | Carbohydrates: 7.6g | Fiber: 2.2g |Protein: 16g

Recipe 46: Asparagus Soup

TIME TO PREPARE
6 minutes

COOK TIME
10 Minutes

SERVING
4 People

Ingredients

- ½ lb of fresh asparagus cut into pieces. Make sure to remove the woody ends of the asparagus.
- 1 Sliced or chopped medium sized yellow onion.
- 3 Chopped or minced cloves of garlic cloves.
- 3 tbsp of coconuts oil.
- ½ teaspoon of dried thyme
- 5 Cups of bone broth
- Zest + 1 Tbsp of juice of organic lemon
- 1 Teaspoon of sea salt
- 2 Cups of organic sour cream*

Instructions

1. Prepare your asparagus, the onion and the garlic. Remove all the woody ends from the asparagus stalks and discard it.
2. Chop the asparagus into pieces of 1 inch each.
3. Slice the onion into halves and chop it.
4. Smash the garlic cloves or chop it.
5. Set the ingredients aside.
6. Place your stainless steel bowl inside your Instant Pot without putting the lid on it.
7. Set your Instant Pot to the button "Sauté" and then add the coconut oil; the add onions and the garlic. Cook the mixture for 5 minutes and keep stirring occasionally; add the thyme and the cook for 1 more minutes.
8. Add the broth, the asparagus and the lemon zest with the salt.
9. Lock the lid of the Instant pot and press the button "Manual" high pressure.
10. Set the pressure timer to 5 minutes and when the timer goes off, add the sour cream and stir; of course after the instant pot releases the steam.
11. Serve and enjoy

Nutrition Information

Calories: 161.2| Fat: 8.2g | Carbohydrates: 16.4g | Fiber: 0.7g |Protein: 6.3g

Recipe 47: Lentil Soup

TIME TO PREPARE
6 minutes

COOK TIME
10 Minutes

SERVING
4 People

Ingredients

- 1 Big diced onion
- 3 minced garlic cloves
- 2 Tbsp of red curry paste
- 1/8 Teaspoon of ginger powder
- 1 Tbsp of red pepper flakes
- 1 and ½ oz Can coconut milk
- 1 oz Can of cut tomatoes
- 2 Cups of broth (Vegetable broth)
- 1 and ½ Cups of Red lentils
- Spinach

Instructions

1. In your Instant Pot cooker, click the button of the option "Sauté" and wait a couple of minutes until it becomes warm.
2. Now, add your diced onion and the garlic; then sauté altogether until the components become brown. Add a little quantity of broth.
3. Once you notice the ingredients starting to have a brown colour, press the cancelling button to stop the process of sautéing.
4. Add the paste of the red curry, the ginger powder and the red pepper flakes and keep stirring.
5. Add your coconut milk, the diced tomatoes, the vegetable broth and the lentils and stir again.
6. Now, lock the lid and the button "Manual" then reduce your timer to around 7 minutes.
7. Let the pressure in the Instant Pot release.
8. Once the steam is released, open the Instant Pot and add the spinach
9. Serve and enjoy your soup.

Nutrition Information

Calories: 120| Fat: 1.5g | Carbohydrates: 20g | Fiber: 7g |Protein: 8g

Recipe 48: Potato Soup

TIME TO PREPARE
5 minutes

COOK TIME
30 Minutes

SERVING
5 People

Ingredients

- 6 medium peeled and diced potatoes
- ¾ Cup of sliced baby carrots
- ½ Can of Progresso Creamy Garlic
- ½ Cup of chopped celery
- ½ Cup of fresh and chopped baby spinach leaves
- 1 Cup of chopped onion
- 1 Cup of broth
- 1/8 Teaspoon of crushed red pepper
- 1/8 Teaspoon of paprika
- 1 Tbsp of ground flax or you can use chia seeds

Instructions

1. Place all of your ingredients inside your Instant Pot and mix them very well.
2. Lock the led and set the button to Soup and set your timer to 30 minutes.
3. When you hear the beep of the Instant Pot, place a towel on the lid and try a fast pressure release; then insert your blender to immerse and keep repeating the same procedure until your soup become thick.
4. Taste your soup and add a pinch of salt if needed.
5. Serve your soup and enjoy it with Serve whole grain wheat bread.

- ½ Teaspoon of salt
- Sharp grated cheddar cheese
- Basil leaves

Nutrition Information

Calories: 208| Fat: 6.1g | Carbohydrates: 28g | Fiber: 1.8g |Protein: 8.3g

Recipe 49: Cauliflower Soup

TIME TO PREPARE
5 minutes

COOK TIME
30 Minutes

SERVING
5 People

Ingredients

- 4 Cups of vegetable broth (Low sodium)
- 1 Head of cubed and chopped cauliflower
- 3 Cups of chopped potatoes
- 4 Cups of onion
- 2 large carrots
- ½ Cup of celery
- 2Tbsp of Raw Coconut Amino.
- 1 Tbsp of Coconuts oil.

Instructions

1. Pour the coconuts oil in the Instant Pot
2. Add all of your ingredients into the Instant Pot you liner you are using.
3. Lock the lid of your Instant Pot; seal the vent of the steam.
4. Press the button "Manual" and "Adjust" the time to 9 minutes of cooking time. Once the pressure is reached, then the countdown starts.
5. Add 2Teaspoons of cashew butter
6. Use the blender to mash the soup and add a few cups of kale for nutritional values
7. Garnish your soup; then ladle in serving bowls
8. Serve and enjoy your soup!

Nutrition Information

Calories: 134| Fat: 8g | Carbohydrates: 12g | Fiber: 5g |Protein: 6g

Recipe 50: Carrot soup with fowl

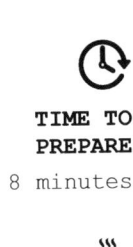

TIME TO PREPARE
8 minutes

COOK TIME
20 Minutes

SERVING
4 People

Ingredients

- ½ fowl or chicken
- 2 quarts of chicken broth
- ¼ Cup of coarsely chopped onion
- ½ Cup of coarsely chopped carrots
- ½ Cup of coarsely chopped celery
- 1 Teaspoon of saffron threads
- ¾ Cup of corn kernels
- ½ Cup of finely chopped celery
- 1 tablespoon of fresh chopped parsley
- 1 Cup of cooked egg noodles

Instructions

1. Start by combining all together the stewing chicken or fowl with the chicken broth in your Instant Pot
2. Press sauté and add the onions, the carrots, the celery and the saffron
3. Now, close the lid of the instant Pot and set at high pressure for around 20 minutes
4. Once the timer beeps, remove the chicken and shred it from the bone and cut it into small pieces
5. Strain your saffron broth with a fine sieve and then add the celery, the corn, the parsley, and the cooked noodles to your broth.
6. Return your soup to simmer for a few minutes
7. Serve and enjoy a delicious and nutritious soup

Nutrition Information

Calories: 154.4| Fat: 0.8g | Carbohydrates: 27.2g | Fiber: 5.1g |Protein: 10.9g

Recipe 51: Instant Pot Angel Hair Soup

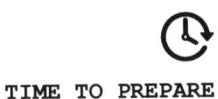

TIME TO PREPARE
5 minutes

COOK TIME
15 Minutes

SERVING
4 People

Ingredients

- 4 Cups of low sodium chicken broth
- 3 Tbsp of tomato sauce
- ½ lb of angel hair pasta
- 7 leaves of fresh basil
- 2 tbsp of olive oil
- ¼ Cup of parmesan cheese to serve
- 2 Peeled and diced carrots
- 1 Peeled and cubed potato
- ¼ Cup of chickpeas

Instructions

1. Pour the oil, and add the broth, the chickpeas, the carrots, the tomato sauce and the basil in your Instant Pot
2. Press sauté and let the ingredients simmer for around 5 minutes.
3. Add 1 and ½ cup of chicken broth or and close the lid of the Instant Pot.
4. Set at high pressure for around 10 minutes.
5. Once the timer beeps, quick release the pressure and stir in the angel's hair pasta.
6. Boil the ingredients for 5 minutes
7. Add the basil and let cook for another minute.
8. Serve in bowl with a sprinkle of Parmesan cheese and tortilla strips.
9. Serve and enjoy!

Nutrition Information

Calories: 216| Fat: 3.8g | Carbohydrates: 35.1g | Fiber: 6g |Protein: 12.4g

Recipe 52: Coconut Lime Soup

TIME TO PREPARE
6 minutes

COOK TIME
10 Minutes

SERVING
3-4 People

Ingredients

- ½ Tbsp of coconut Oil
- 1 Finely chopped onion
- 1 Teaspoon of ground coriander powder
- 1 Medium sized Cauliflower that are broken into large floret
- 3 Cups of Vegetable Broth
- ½ Cup of Coconut Milk
- 2-3 Tbsp of Lime Juice
- 1 Pinch of Salt to taste

Instructions

1. Start by heating the Instant Pot and set the Manual button to sauté mode and sauté the onion for 6 minutes.
2. Add the coriander and keep stirring for a couple of minutes.
3. Add the rest of the ingredients; from the cauliflower, the vegetable broth and the coconut milk; then stir the ingredients to combine them.
4. Lock the lid and set the timer to 10 minutes.
5. Once the timer sets off; press the button keep warm and release the pressure
6. Blend the ingredients with a blender until it becomes soft
7. Add the lime juice and adjust the salt to taste
8. Serve and enjoy your soup!

Nutrition Information

Calories: 262.8| Fat: 12.7g | Carbohydrates: 16g | Fiber: 1.3g |Protein: 22g

Recipe 53: Garlic Soup with Almonds

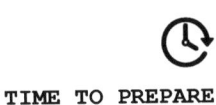

TIME TO PREPARE
5 minutes

COOK TIME
15 Minutes

SERVING
3 People

Ingredients

- 3 and ¼ cups of freezing water
- 2 and ¼ cups of blanched almonds
- 5 Peeled and minced cloves of garlic
- 1 Baguette (remove the crusts removed and cut it into pieces)
- ½ Cup of coconuts oil
- 2 And ½ tbsp of sherry vinegar
- 2 Drops of almond extract
- 1 Pinch of Kosher salt

Instructions

1. Start by combining the 2 cups of water in the Instant Processor with the almonds, the garlic, and the bread in the food processor.
2. Set the manual to the button Sauté; sauté the ingredients soften for around 5 minutes.
3. Add the remaining quantity of water, the coconut oil, the vinegar, the extract, and the salt.
4. Cancel the setting of the Sauté feature and set the timer to 10 minutes
5. Once the timer is off, release the pressure and blend the ingredients with the a food processor or blender
6. Garnish your soup with the halves of almonds.
7. Serve and enjoy your soup!

Nutrition Information

Calories: 120| Fat: 13.4g | Carbohydrates: 37.1g | Fiber: 9.6g |Protein: 7.1g

Recipe 54: Beef Noodle Soup

TIME TO PREPARE
8 minutes

COOK TIME
35 Minutes

SERVING
4 People

Ingredients

- ½ lb of beef shoulder
- 1 Tbsp of kosher salt
- ¼ Cup of fresh ground black pepper
- ½ Teaspoon of all spice
- ¼ Teaspoon of ground ginger
- 1 Tbsp of coconut oil
- 1 Piece of 1 inch of fresh ginger
- 4 Cups of chicken broth
- ¼ Cups of fish sauce
- 1 Medium head of bok choy
- 1 Head of cabbage
- 1 or 2 packages of Shriataki noodles
- 2 scallions
- ¼ Cup of cilantro
- 1 Cup of bean sprouts

Instructions

1. Cut the beef into one and small cubes of 1 inch each.
2. Blend all together the salt, the pepper, the all spice powder and the ginger.
3. Spice the quantity of beef cubes into the mixture of the spices.
4. Set your Instant pot to the feature sauté, and once it becomes hot; then stir in the beef and sauté it until it becomes brown.
5. Add the broth of chicken
6. Add the fish sauce and the ginger
7. Now, lock the lid over the Instant Pot and set your Instant Pot to the Beef. Feature Stew and cook it for around 30 minutes. Meanwhile; cut the bok choy, the Napa cabbage and the scallions
8. When the cooking process is complete and the timer of the Instant Pot gets off, vent your steam and remove its lid. Then set the feature of the Instant Pot to the mode sauté
9. Add the Napa cabbage, the bok choy and the scallion; then simmer for around 5 minutes
10. Drain your noodles and rinse it; then add it to your

instant Pot. Let the ingredients simmer for around 2 minutes
11. Serve and enjoy your soup with cilantro for garnish and sprouts

Nutrition Information

Calories: 204.4| Fat: 7.5g | Carbohydrates: 27.8g | Fiber: 1.8g |Protein: 11.7g

Recipe 55: Lamb Stew

TIME TO PREPARE
10 minutes

COOK TIME
35 Minutes

SERVING
5-6 People

Ingredients

- 2 lbs of diced lamb stew meat
- 1 Large acorn squash
- 4 Medium carrots
- 2 Small yellow onions
- 2 Rosemary Sprigs.
- 1 bay leaf
- 6 sliced or minced cloves of garlic
- 3 Tbsp of broth or water
- ¼ Tbsp of sp salt (Adjust it to taste)

Instructions

1. Start by peeling and seeding, then cubing your acorn squash. You can use a nice trick which is to microwave the squash for 2 minutes.
2. Slice the carrots into quite thick circles.
3. Peel your onions and cut it into halves; then slice it into the shape of half moons.
4. Now, place all of your ingredients in the Instant Pot and set the feature Soup/ Stew button.
5. Lock the lid and set the timer to 35 minutes.
6. When the timer goes off; release the steam and pressure before opening the lid.
7. Serve and enjoy your stew.

Nutrition Information

Calories: 332.7| Fat: 6.9g | Carbohydrates: 38.9g | Fiber: 6.4g |Protein: 28.9g

CHAPTER 6: SEAFOOD AND POULTRY RECIPES

RECIPE 56: SALMON WITH MANGO SALSA

TIME TO PREPARE
4-5 minutes

COOK TIME
10 Minutes

SERVING
3 People

Ingredients

- 2 Fillet of salmon
- ½ Lemon juice
- 1 pinch of salt
- 1 pinch of pepper
- 1 pinch of ginger
- Juice of 1/2 lemon
- For your Salsa made of Mango & Pomegranate
- 1 Cubed and ripe mango
- 1 Medium lime
- 2 Finely chopped medium green onions
- 1 Handful of chopped coriander
- Salt
- ½ Chopped red pepper
- 6 Finely cut slices of Jalapeno
- 4 Tbsp of

Instructions

1. Turn on your Instant Pot by pressing the setting "sauté"
2. Pour in the oil
3. Add the fillets of the salmon above a baking sheet
4. Season the salmon with the lemon juice, the salt and the pepper
5. Close your pressure cooker and set the pressing the function Sauté
6. Pressure cook for around 10 minutes or until they are perfectly cooked
7. Meanwhile and in a separate bowl, mix all together the ingredients of the salsa.
8. And once your salmon is ready, quick release the pressure; then when it is safe to do, open the lid and serve the salmon
9. Serve with the mango and pomegranate salsa!

pomegranate seeds

Nutrition Information

Calories: 542.7| Fat: 20.2g | Carbohydrates: 46.2 g | Fiber: 2.8g |Protein: 43.8g

Recipe 57: Salmon with Lemon Wedges

TIME TO PREPARE
6 minutes

COOK TIME
20 Minutes

SERVING
2-3 People

Ingredients

- 2 Fillet of salmon
- ½ Lemon juice
- 1 pinch of salt
- 1 pinch of pepper
- 1 pinch of ginger
- Juice of 1/2 lemon
- For your Salsa made of Mango & Pomegranate
- 1 Cubed and ripe mango
- 1 Medium lime
- 2 Finely chopped medium green onions
- 1 Handful of chopped coriander
- Salt
- ½ Chopped red

Instructions

1. In your Instant Pot, pour the olive oil and heat it by pressing the Sauté function feature.
2. Add the lime zest, the lime juice and the garlic; the, season with the salt and the pepper.
3. Add the salmon in and sauté it for around 10 minutes. Be careful not to stir too much, the salmon is fragile
4. Once the Salmon is perfectly cooked; remove it from the Instant Pot and prepare the coconut rice
5. Pour the coconut water, the coconut milk, the rice and the salt in the Instant Pot and press the featuring setting Boil or soup.
6. Close the lid of the Instant Pot and seal the valve. Set the time to 20 minutes at high pressure.
7. Meanwhile, prepare the avocado-mango salsa:
8. Take a bowl of a medium size and toss in it the mango, the bell pepper and the cilantro with the red onion and the avocadoo
9. Add the lime juice, the olive oil and then the

pepper
- 6 Finely cut slices of Jalapeno
- 4 Tbsp of pomegranate seeds

coconut water. Then season the mixture with the salt and the pepper.
10. Once you hear the timer of the Instant Pot beeps; quick release the pressure. Serve and enjoy your salmons with the avocado Mango salsa and the coconut rice.
11. Serve salmon warm with coconut rice top with avocado mango salsa.

Nutrition Information

Calories: 270.7| Fat: 11.5g | Carbohydrates: 14.2 g | Fiber: 1.4g |Protein: 28.1g

Recipe 58: Salmon with Asparagus

Time to Prepare
6 minutes

Cook Time
20 Minutes

Serving
2-3 People

Ingredients

- Tbsp of coconut oil
- 1 Diced yellow onion
- 2 Minced garlic cloves
- 13 Spears of cut asparagus
- 1 Cup of dried and sprouted trio quinoa
- ½ Cup of crumbled feta cheese
- 1 Tbsp of chia seeds
- ⅓ Cup of slivered almonds
- 1 and ½ Cup of fresh spinach leaves
- 2 Diced and hard boiled eggs
- 2 Tbsp of diced parsley
- 1 Medium lemon
- ½ Cup of olive oil
- 1 pinch of kosher salt

Instructions

1. Heat your Instant Pot over a medium heat and pour 1 Tbsp of coconut oil into it.
2. Add the salmon and sprinkle above it the cayenne pepper and the seasoning of the lemon and the pepper.
3. Squeeze around ½ of the lemon over the top of the salmon. ½ of lemon over top and set the featuring function to 8 to 10 minutes.
4. When the salmon is perfectly cooked, remove it from the Instant Pot and set it aside.
5. Now, melt 1 Tbsp of coconut oil. Then add the cut onions and then cook the mixture for around 5 minutes. Sprinkle a little bit of salt.
6. Add the garlic and then keep stirring for around 30 seconds to heat it
7. Add the asparagus spears and sauté the ingredients for about 5 minutes.
8. Add the salmon to the ingredient for 2 minutes; meanwhile, cook the quinoa in a separate medium saucepan of a quantity of boiling water; then add 1 pinch of salt and let it simmer for 13 minutes.
9. When your quinoa is cooked, remove it from the

- 1 pinch of pepper
- 1 and ½ lb of skinned salmon
- ¼ Teaspoon of cayenne pepper
- ¼ Teaspoon of lemon pepper for seasoning

heat and then add the spinach to top your quinoa put and cook for 2 more minutes.

10. Add the spinach and the quinoa to the asparagus and the salmon. Add the chia seeds, the lemon juice, the olive oil, the almonds, the feta cheese, the parsley, the egg and the salt with the pepper to the Salmon and the asparagus.
11. Serve and enjoy your salmon dish!

Nutrition Information

Calories: 245.6| Fat: 6g | Carbohydrates: 12.2 g | Fiber: 5.64g |Protein: 141.1g

Recipe 59: Shrimp with Mango

TIME TO PREPARE
5 minutes

COOK TIME
6 Minutes

SERVING
3 People

Ingredients

- 1 lb of shelled and deveined jumbo shrimps
- 2 Teaspoons of extra coconut oil
- ¼ Teaspoon of salt
- 3 Minced cloves of garlic
- 2 Cut scallions into segments of 2 inch each
- 3 Slices of julienned ginger
- 1 Tbsp of vegetable oil
- 4 Peeled and diagonally sliced carrots
- 3 Peeled and sliced broccoli stems
- ¼ Cup of chicken broth (Low sodium)

Instructions

1. Prepare all of your ingredients.
2. Combine the ingredients of your shrimps in a medium bowl.
3. Heat your Instant Pot. Pour 1 Tbsp of coconut oil and then add the shrimps to the Instant Pot.
1. Line your shrimps in just 1 layer and press the Sauté feature function.
2. Sauté the shrimps for 2 minutes
3. Meanwhile, flip the shrimp occasionally to each side.
4. Once your shrimp become pink, remove it from the Instant Pot and set it aside.
5. Add the vegetable oil without removing the juice of the shrimps.
6. Add the rest of the vegetables and pour 1 cup of water with a little bit of salt.
7. Close the lid and boil at high pressure for 5 minutes.
8. One the timer beeps, add the shrimps and the chunks of the mango.
9. Mix the ingredients very well and cook for 1 minute.
10. Serve and enjoy your shrimp with rice.

- ½ Teaspoon or a pinch of salt
- 2 Firm, peeled and cut mangoes

Nutrition Information

Calories: 223.1| Fat: 4.3g | Carbohydrates: 29.2 g | Fiber: 4.4g |Protein: 19.5g

RECIPE 60: SHRIMP DUMPLINGS

TIME TO PREPARE
10 minutes

COOK TIME
5 Minutes

SERVING
5 People

Ingredients

- 10 oz of finely cut shrimp meat
- 1 Tbsp of grated ginger
- 1 Tbsp of lemon juice
- 1 Tbsp of cilantro (Finely chopped)
- 1 teaspoon of coconut oil
- Around 20 dumpling or you can use wonton wrappers
- 2 Cups of shrimp stock
- 3 Minced garlic cloves
- For the dipping sauce; 1/4 cup of lemon juice + 2 Tbsp of chili sauce
- 1 Tbsp of sugar

Instructions

1. Place your Instant Pot over a medium high heat and pour 1 cup of stock in it.
2. In a bow, place your shrimp meat, the ginger, the lemon juice and the coconut oil; then mix the ingredients to combine it very well.
3. Pour 1 Tbsp of your mixture on a wonton wrapper or a dumpling; then brush each of the edges with the use of water.
4. Finally, press the dumplings edges and seal it.
5. Line the dumplings in the Instant Pot and press the setting feature to Boil and set the timer to 5 minutes at high pressure. (Use a medium high heat)
6. You can cook the dumplings in batches and when you finish cooking,
7. Meanwhile, you can prepare the dipping sauce by

mixing the lemon juice; the chili sauce and the sugar.

8. Serve and enjoy your dumplings.

Nutrition Information

Calories: 130| Fat: 2.5g | Carbohydrates: 17 g | Fiber: 1g |Protein: 7g

Recipe 61: Tilapia with Lemon slices

TIME TO PREPARE
6 minutes

COOK TIME
15 Minutes

SERVING
3-4 People

Ingredients

- 1/2 lb of fillets tilapia
- 2 Teaspoons of coconut oil
- 3 Tbsp of Chia seeds
- ¼ Teaspoon of Old Bay Seasoning
- ½ Teaspoon of garlic
- ½ Teaspoon of salt
- 1 Large and sliced lemon
- 1 teaspoon of grated and fresh ginger
- 1 Package of frozen cauliflower with red pepper and broccoli and red pepper

Instructions

1. Place your Instant Pot on a low heat and pour the coconut oil in it.
2. Press the setting Sauté and wait until the coconut oil melts to put the tilapia fillets into the bottom of your Instant Pot.
3. Season the tilapia with the seasoning of the Old Bay and the garlic; the ginger, the salt and then sprinkle chia seeds. Now, top each of the salmon pieces with the use of a slice or two of lemons. Arrange your frozen vegetables around the portions of fish, and season it with the salt and the pepper.
4. Cover the lid of the Instant Pot and set it to high pressure for 10 to 15 minutes dish.
5. Once the timer goes off, quick release the pressure and serve you lunch
6. Enjoy a delicious dish!

Nutrition Information

Calories: 200.5| Fat: 13.3g | Carbohydrates: 2.3 g | Fiber: 0.6g |Protein: 21g

Recipe 62: Fish with Celery and Potatoes

TIME TO PREPARE
5 minutes

COOK TIME
8 Minutes

SERVING
4 People

Ingredients

- 2 leeks of celery stalks
- 2 Carrots
- 1 and ½ lbs of potatoes
- 2 Tbsp of coconut oil
- ½ Cup of button mushrooms
- 2 and ½ cup of hot fish stock
- ½ lb of white fish fillet (skinless)
- ½ lb of skinless salmon fillet
- 1 Tbsp of chopped fresh tarragon
- 2 Tbsp of chopped fresh parsley
- ¼ Cup of mayonnaise
- ¼ Cup of plain yogurt
- 2 minced garlic cloves

Instructions

1. Place your Instant Pot on a medium high heat and pour the oil in it.
2. Put the leek in the Instant Pot with the cut celery and the cubes of carrot.
3. Press the setting sauté and reduce the heat. Close the lid of the Instant pot and cook the ingredients for around 3 minutes.
4. Add your diced potatoes and the mushrooms to your Instant pot and then pour the hot stock.
5. Press the setting boil and cover the lid; then press high pressure for 5 minutes.
6. Meanwhile, cut your salmon and fish into cubes.
7. Once the timer beeps, quick release the pressure and add your white fish with the salmon Simmer the ingredients again; then cover close the lid of the Instant Pot and cook the mixture for 5 more minutes.
8. In the meantime, combine the mayonnaise with the yogurt, the garlic, the paprika and the chilli powder.
9. Add the tarragon and the parsley into your casserole before placing it into four large bowls.

- ½ Teaspoon of paprika
- 1 Pinch of chilli powder
- 1 baguette

10. Serve your dish with the yogurt and the toasted slices of the baguette.

Nutrition Information

Calories: 304| Fat: 10.4g | Carbohydrates: 27.6 g | Fiber: 9.2g |Protein: 20.4g

Recipe 63: Fish with Strawberries and Kiwi

TIME TO PREPARE
6 minutes

COOK TIME
8 Minutes

SERVING
3 People

Ingredients

- 5-5 oz of fillet fish (You can use 4 oz from each the white fish, the sole or the red fish)
- 2 Tbsp of chili powder
- 2 Teaspoons of garlic powder
- 2 Teaspoons of cumin
- 2 Teaspoons of paprika
- ½ Teaspoon of salt
- 2 Tbsp of coconut oil
- ¼ teaspoon of ground ginger
- For the Salsa of the Strawberry and Kiwi:
- 1 and ½ cup of strawberry cubes

Instructions

1. Start your Instant Pot by pressing the setting function "sauté" on a medium heat and melt the coconut oil in it.
2. Press the setting feature sauté and add the fish.
3. Stir in the garlic powder, the chilli powder, the ginger powder, the cumin, the paprika and the salt.
4. Make sure that your fish is evenly coated and cook the fish for around 5 minutes with the lid off or you can set high pressure for three minutes.
5. Flip your fish one or two times in the process and cook for 3 more minutes.
6. For your Strawberry and Kiwi Salsa:
7. Combine all of your ingredients into a bowl and toss them together.
8. Sprinkle the toasted almonds over the salsa
9. Serve your fish with the salsa and enjoy!

- 1 Diced and peeled
- ½ Cucumber cut into cubes
- 2 Tbsp of chopped fresh cilantro
- 2 Teaspoons of lemon juice
- ¼ Cup of sliced onion (Red)
- ¼ Minced and seeded jalapeño
- ¼ Cup of toasted and chopped Almonds

Nutrition Information

Calories: 242.4| Fat: 9.4g | Carbohydrates: 19.2 g | Fiber: 6.7g |Protein: 21.8g

Recipe 64: Halibut with Blueberries

TIME TO PREPARE
6 minutes

COOK TIME
8 Minutes

SERVING
3 People

Ingredients

- 4 Steaks of Halibut steaks
- 4 Purple potatoes
- Arugula and Romaine with spinach for the salad
- 1 and ½ cup of frozen and fresh blueberries
- 2 Tbsp of honey or brown sugar
- 1 Tbsp of coconut
- Zest of 1 or ½ a lime
- ½ Squeezed lime
- 1 Pinch of hot sauce
- 1 Pinch of black pepper
- 1 Pinch of flax seeds powder
- 2 Chopped mint sprigs
- 2 Tbsp of fresh basil
- 1 Pinch of salt
- 1 Pinch of pepper

Instructions

1. Cut your fish into cubes or small pieces.
2. Clean, the drain your fish very well
3. Place your Instant Pot over a medium heat and pour the coconut oil in it.
4. Wait until the oil melts; then add the fish to the Instant Pot and add to it the fish with the salt, the pepper and the ginger and press the function sauté to sauté your fish for 5 minutes.
5. Once cooked, remove the fish from the Instant Pot.
6. Add the blueberries to the Instant Pot, the lime zest, the sugar or the honey, the mint, the pepper, the ginger, the mint, the basil, the flax seeds powder and the potatoes. Then pour around 1 cup of water into the mixture and press the function Boil or soup.
7. Close the lid of the Instant Pot and set high pressure for 5 minutes.
8. Once the timer beeps, quick release the pressure and check if the mixture became thick, if not, cook for a 5 more minutes.
9. Serve and enjoy your fish with lime wedges, blueberries and the potatoes

- 2 to 3 Tbsp of coconut oil

Nutrition Information

Calories: 127.2| Fat: 5.7g | Carbohydrates: 1g | Fiber: 0.0g |Protein: 16.7g

Recipe 65: Scallops with Strawberry Salsa

TIME TO PREPARE
5 minutes

COOK TIME
5 Minutes

SERVING
3-4 People

Ingredients

- 1 Cup of strawberries (Ripe)
- ½ Minced shallot
- 2 Tbsp of minced arugula and basil
- 1 Tbsp of red wine vinegar
- ½ lb of scallops (remove the tough membrane)
- 1 pinch of salt
- 1 pinch of pepper
- ¼ Cup of toasted and chopped almonds
- 1 Tbsp of chia butter
- 1 Tbsp of coconut oil
- Arugula and basil leaves.
- 1 Pinch of salt
- 1 Pinch of pepper
- 1 Pinch of ginger

Instructions

1. Start by combining the strawberries, the shallot, the vinegar and the minced arugula with the basil in a bowl.
2. Add the salt and the pepper to taste.
3. Adjust the seasoning until you taste a balanced and nice tasted between the sweet and the sour. (You may need to add a little bit more of sugar)
4. Place your Instant Pot over a medium heat
5. Pour the butter and the coconut oil and press the button sauté
6. When the oil is melted, reduce the heat and add your scallops carefully.
7. Season the scallops with the salt, the pepper and the ginger
8. Sauté the scallops for around 3 minutes without flipping it
9. After 3 minutes, flip your scallops and cook for 2 more minutes
10. Once cooked, remove the scallops from the heat and top each one of the Strawberries salsa.
11. Serve and garnish with the basil and the arugula; then sprinkle the almonds.

Nutrition Information

Calories: 392| Fat: 8.9g | Carbohydrates: 45.5g | Fiber: 4.2g |Protein: 33.2g

RECIPE 66: MAHI MAHI WITH AVOCADO SALSA

TIME TO PREPARE
6 minutes

COOK TIME
7 Minutes

SERVING
3 People

Ingredients

- 4 filets of mahi-mahi
- 1 Tbsp of butter
- 2 Tbsp of coconut oil
- 3 Tbsp of Cajun seasoning
- 2 Teaspoon of kosher salt
- For your Strawberry and Avocado Salsa:
- ½ Cup of hulled and cubed pint strawberries
- 1 Large and diced avocado
- ½ Finely sliced red onion
- 1 Seeded and cubed jalapeno
- ¼ Cup of chopped cilantro
- ½ orange (juice)

Instructions

1. Start your Instant Pot by pressing the setting function sauté; then melt the coconut oil.
2. Season both sides of your fish with the salt and the Cajun.
3. When the coconut oil melts, lay your fish and cook it for around 4 minutes.
4. Flip your fish and cook for around 3 minutes
5. When you notice that the muscles of the fish begin to pull away, you'll know that it is perfectly cooked.
6. Remove the fish from the Instant Pot and make the salsa by combining all of your ingredients into a bowl.
7. Season the salsa with the salt.
8. Serve your fish filets with the salsa!

- ½ Of a lemon
- 1 Pinch of kosher salt

Nutrition Information

RECIPE 67: HADDOCK FISH WITH SWEET POTATOES

TIME TO PREPARE
5 minutes

COOK TIME
10 Minutes

SERVING
3 People

Ingredients

- 1lb of wild caught Haddock or white fish
- 2 Tbsp of ghee butter or you can use coconut oil
- 1 Medium finely chopped onion
- 1 Chopped carrot
- 1 Large red peeled and cubed potato
- 1 Minced garlic clove
- 2 Cups of chicken broth
- 2 Cups of whole Peeled Tomatoes
- 1 Pinch of crushed red pepper flakes
- 2 Teaspoons of sea salt
- ½ Teaspoon of black pepper
- 2 Cups of chopped packed kale
- ½ Cup of heavy cream or coconut cream
- 2 Tbsp of freshly chopped parsley

Instructions

1. Pour 1tbsp of vegetable oil or ghee in your Instant Pot and sauté the onion and the garlic for around 4 minutes.
2. Add the chicken stock, the cubed carrots and the potatoes, the chopped herbs and the peeled and chopped tomatoes.
3. Simmer the ingredients for around 5 minutes.
4. Line your haddock filets on the top of your steaming rack.
5. Sprinkle with salt and pepper; then close the lid of the Instant Pot and cook for around 6 minutes.
6. Once the timer beeps, quick release the pressure.
7. Blend the veggies in a food processor; then add the kale, the cream and the fish.
8. Serve and enjoy a light healthy fish dish!

- 1Tbsp of freshly chopped basil

Nutrition Information

Calories: 287| Fat: 8g | Carbohydrates: 26g | Fiber: 6g |Protein: 24g

Recipe 68: Swordfish with Herbs and Pineapple salsa

TIME TO PREPARE
5 minutes

COOK TIME
10 Minutes

SERVING
4 People

Ingredients

- 1 lb of swordfish steak
- 2 Tbsp of extra virgin olive oil
- 1 Pinch of kosher salt and 1 pinch of freshly ground black pepper
- 4 Tbsp of butter
- 1 Teaspoon of smoked paprika
- 4 Sprigs of rosemary

To prepare the salsa

- ½ Cup of diced pineapple
- ¼ Cup of diced cantaloupe
- ⅛ Cup of red minced onion
- ½ Of diced avocado
- 1 and ½ of minced jalapeño

Instructions

1. For the salsa, mix all together the fruits with the jalapeño, the lime and the herbs into deep bowl and then season it with the kosher salt according to your taste.
2. Add the lime juice to the sauce if you desire and set it aside in the refrigerator.
3. Now, rinse the swordfish and pat it dry with the help of paper towels.
4. Oil the fish and season it with the kosher salt and the freshly ground black pepper.
5. Pour 1 cup of water in the Instant Pot and place the trivet in its place.
6. Take a baking tray that fits the Instant Pot and grease it with butter.
7. Place the fish in the baking dish and add to it the rosemary sprigs and the paprika.
8. Cover the baking dish with an aluminum sling foil and place it on the trivet.
9. Close the lid of the Instant Pot and set at high pressure for around 10 minutes.

- ½ of juiced lime
- ¼ Cup of chopped cilantro
- 1 Tbsp of chopped mint
- 1 Tbsp of minced rosemary
- 1 Pinch of kosher salt

10. Once the timer beeps, quick release the pressure.
11. Add more paprika and butter; then serve it with fruit salsa!

Nutrition Information

Calories: 450.6| Fat: 20.5g | Carbohydrates: 18g | Fiber: 4.1g |Protein: 51.7g

Recipe 69: Cod Fish with cauliflower Rice

TIME TO PREPARE
4 minutes

COOK TIME
10 Minutes

SERVING
3 People

Ingredients

- Cauliflower Rice
- 1 large bunch of lacinato kale, stems removed, chopped (make my smoky kale stems with leftovers)
- 1 small leek, cleaned and cut into thin rings
- 1 pound of wild cod pieces (I buy mine from here)
- 1-1/2 tablespoons of coconut oil
- 1/2 fresh lemon
- 1 Pinch of salt
- 1 Pinch of pepper to taste

Instructions

1. Place 1/2 tablespoon of coconut oil in the instant pot. Add the leeks and sauté until translucent, and then add the kale.
2. Season with salt and pepper and cover the lid and set the timer for 8 minutes and the pressure to "high" until the kale is nearly cooked through
3. When the timer beeps, quick release the pressure
4. Add the cooked cauliflower rice to the kale and mix. Adjust seasoning if necessary.
5. While the vegetables cook, add one tablespoon of coconut oil to another large pan. Pat the cod dry and season with salt and pepper. When the pan is warm, place the cod inside
6. Cook for about 2 minutes and then flip. When cooked through, squeeze the fresh lemon juice on top.
7. Place the cauliflower kale mixture in a bowl and top with sautéed cod!

Nutrition Information

Calories: 179.3| Fat: 3g | Carbohydrates: 22.5g | Fiber: 3.3g |Protein: 16.6g

Recipe 70: Cod Fish with cauliflower Rice

TIME TO PREPARE
4 minutes

COOK TIME
10 Minutes

SERVING
3 People

Ingredients

- Cauliflower Rice
- 1 large bunch of lacinato kale, stems removed, chopped (make my smoky kale stems with leftovers)
- 1 small leek, cleaned and cut into thin rings
- 1 pound of wild cod pieces (I buy mine from here)
- 1-1/2 tablespoons of coconut oil
- 1/2 fresh lemon
- 1 Pinch of salt
- 1 Pinch of pepper to taste

Instructions

8. Place 1/2 tablespoon of coconut oil in the instant pot. Add the leeks and sauté until translucent, and then add the kale.
9. Season with salt and pepper and cover the lid and set the timer for 8 minutes and the pressure to "high" until the kale is nearly cooked through
10. When the timer beeps, quick release the pressure
11. Add the cooked cauliflower rice to the kale and mix. Adjust seasoning if necessary.
12. While the vegetables cook, add one tablespoon of coconut oil to another large pan. Pat the cod dry and season with salt and pepper. When the pan is warm, place the cod inside
13. Cook for about 2 minutes and then flip. When cooked through, squeeze the fresh lemon juice on top.
14. Place the cauliflower kale mixture in a bowl and top with sautéed cod!

Nutrition Information

Calories: 179.3| Fat: 3g | Carbohydrates: 22.5g | Fiber: 3.3g |Protein: 16.6g

RECIPE 71: SALMON WITH BASIL AND DILL

TIME TO PREPARE
5 minutes

COOK TIME
5 Minutes

SERVING
3 People

Ingredients

- ¾ cup water
- A few sprigs of parsley dill, tarragon, basil or a combo
- 1 pound salmon filet skin on
- 3 teaspoons ghee or other healthy fat divided
- ¼ teaspoon salt or to taste
- ½ teaspoon pepper or to taste
- 1/2 lemon thinly sliced
- 1 Peeled carrot; julienned

Instructions

1. Put water and herbs in the Instant Pot and then put in the steamer rack making sure the handles are extended up.
2. Place salmon, skin down on rack.
3. Drizzle salmon with ghee/fat, season with salt and pepper, and cover with lemon slices.
4. Close the Instant Pot and make sure vent is turned to "Sealing". Plug it in, press "Steam" and press the + or – buttons to set it to 3 minutes.
5. While salmon cooks, julienne the carrots.
6. When the Instant Pot beeps that it's done, quick release the pressure
7. Press the "Warm/Cancel" button. Remove lid, and using hot pads, carefully remove rack with salmon and set on a plate.
8. Remove herbs and discard. Add the carrots and put the lid back on. Press "Sauté" and let the veggies cook for just 1 or 2 minutes.
9. Serve with salmon and add remaining teaspoon of fat to the pot and pour a little of the sauce over them if desired.

Nutrition Information

Calories: 118.1| Fat: 6.8g | Carbohydrates: 1g | Fiber: 0.2g |Protein: 12.9g

RECIPE 72: SEAFOOD GUMBO

TIME TO PREPARE
5 minutes

COOK TIME
10 Minutes

SERVING
3-4 People

Ingredients

- 24 ounces sea bass filets patted dry and cut into 2" chunks
- 3 tablespoons ghee or avocado oil
- 3 tablespoons Cajun seasoning or Creole seasoning
- 2 yellow onions diced
- 2 bell peppers diced
- 4 celery ribs diced
- 28 ounces deseeded and peeled diced tomatoes
- 1/4 cup tomato paste
- 3 bay leaves
- 1 1/2 cups bone broth
- 2 pounds medium to large raw shrimp deveined
- sea salt to taste
- black pepper to taste

Instructions

1. Season the barramundi with some salt and pepper, and make sure they are as evenly coated as possible. Sprinkle half of the Cajun seasoning onto the fish and give it a stir- make sure it is coated well and set aside.
2. Put the ghee in the Instant Pot and push "Sauté". Wait until it reads "Hot" and add the barramundi chunks. Sauté for about 4 minutes, until it looks cooked on both sides. Use a slotted spoon to transfer the fish to a large plate.
3. Add the onions, pepper, celery and the rest of the Cajun seasoning to the pot and sauté for 2 minutes until fragrant. Push "Keep Warm/Cancel". Add the cooked fish, diced tomatoes, tomato paste, bay leaves and bone broth to the pot and give it a nice stir. Put the lid back on the pot and set it to "Sealing." Push "Manual" and set the time for just 5 minutes! The Instant Pot will slowly build up to a high pressure point and once it reaches that point, the gumbo will cook for 5 minutes.
4. Once the 5 minutes have ended, push the "Keep warm/Cancel" button. Cautiously change the "Sealing"

5. valve over to "Venting," which will manually release all of the pressure. Once the pressure has been release (this will take a couple of minutes)
5. Remove the lid and change the setting to "Sauté" again. Add the shrimp and cook for about 3-4 minutes, or until the shrimp have become opaque.
6. Add some more sea salt and black pepper, to taste.
7. Serve hot and top off with some cauliflower rice and chives.

Nutrition Information

Calories: 141.75| Fat: 4.5g | Carbohydrates: 13g | Fiber: 1g |Protein: 5g

RECIPE 73: SHRIMP PAELLA

TIME TO PREPARE
5 minutes

COOK TIME
10 Minutes

SERVING
3-4 People

Ingredients

- 3 Tbsp of Dijon mustard
- 3 Tbsp of melted butter
- 5 teaspoons of honey
- ½ Cup of fresh bread crumbs
- ½ Cup of finely chopped pecans
- 3 Teaspoons of chopped fresh parsley
- 6 Fillets of salmon
- 1 Pinch of salt
- 1 Pinch of pepper
- 6 lemon wedges

Instructions

- 1 pound of frozen wild caught shrimp, 16-20 count shell & tail on
- 1 cup white Rice
- 1/4 cup Organic coconut oil, melted
- 1/4 cup Fresh organic parsley, chopped
- 1 teaspoon Sea Salt
- 1/4 teaspoon Black Pepper
- 1 pinch Crushed Red Pepper Flakes or to taste
- 1 medium lemon, juiced
- 1 pinch saffron
- 1 1/2 cups Water, filtered or chicken broth
- 4 cloves Garlic minced or pressed
- Optional Garnishes
- Organic Grass-Fed Butter
- grated hard cheese parmesan, Romano or Asiago
- Fresh organic parsley, chopped
- lemon, juiced

Nutrition Information

Calories: 157.9| Fat: 4.5g | Carbohydrates: 19.6g | Fiber: 3.5g |Protein: 13.4g

CHAPTER 7: BEEF, LAMB AND PORK RECIPES

Recipe 74: Braised Pork

TIME TO PREPARE
5 minutes

COOK TIME
15 Minutes

SERVING
3-4 People

Ingredients

- 2 lbs of boneless Pork Chops
- ½ Teaspoons of Sea Salt
- ¼ Teaspoons of Black Pepper
- ¼ Cups of Honey
- 2 Tbsp of Dijon Mustard
- ½ Tbsp of Maple Syrup
- ½ Teaspoons of peeled and minced Ginger
- ½ Teaspoons of Cinnamon

Instructions

1. Sprinkle the pork chops with the salt and the pepper and then place it in your Instant Pot.
2. Set the featuring function to sauté and purée your ingredient for around 10 minutes.
3. Take a bowl and mix in it the honey with the Dijon mustard, the maple syrup, the ginger and the cinnamon with the cloves.
4. Pour the honey glaze over the pork chops in the Instant Pot.
5. Lock the lid and set at high pressure for around 15 minutes.
6. Naturally release the pressure for around 5 minutes and then quick release the remaining pressure.
7. Serve and enjoy your dish!

- ¼ Teaspoons of ground garlic cloves

Nutrition Information

Calories: 454| Fat: 2g | Carbohydrates: 44g | Fiber: 0 g |Protein: 7g

RECIPE 75: INSTANT POT GROUND MEAT CASSEROLE

TIME TO PREPARE
8 minutes

COOK TIME
35 Minutes

SERVING
4 People

Ingredients

- 1 lb / 450 g ground beef
- 1 lb / 450 g ground pork
- ¼ cup minced fresh parsley (divided)
- 2 tablespoons dried chopped onion
- 1 teaspoon dried sage
- ½ teaspoon ground mace
- ½ teaspoon sea salt
- 2 cups sliced mushrooms (button or Crimini)
- 1 large onion, chopped
- ½ cup bone broth (or coconut milk, or water)
- 3 tablespoons coconut aminos

Instructions

1. In a bowl, mix together ground beef, pork, 3 tablespoons minced parsley, dried onion, sage, mace, and salt. Once thoroughly mixed, form into meatballs about 1-inch in diameter.

2. Place mushrooms, onion, broth/coconut milk/water, and coconut aminos into the Instant Pot. Add the meatballs.

3. Close and lock the lid. Press the MEAT/STEW button and set cooking time to 35 minutes. Once the time is up, quick release the pressure.

4. Using a slotted spoon gently remove meatballs and transfer to a serving platter.

5. Using an immersion blender or a high-speed blender, purée the cooked mushrooms, onions, and broth into a nice creamy gravy. If the gravy is too thick, add a little more bone broth/coconut

milk/water until the right consistency is reached.

6. Pour gravy over meatballs and garnish with remaining tablespoon of minced parsley

Nutrition Information

Calories: 406.5| Fat: 17.9g | Carbohydrates: 41.2g | Fiber: 5.6 g |Protein: 17.4g

Recipe 76: Instant Pot Short Beef Ribs

TIME TO PREPARE
10 minutes

COOK TIME
30 Minutes

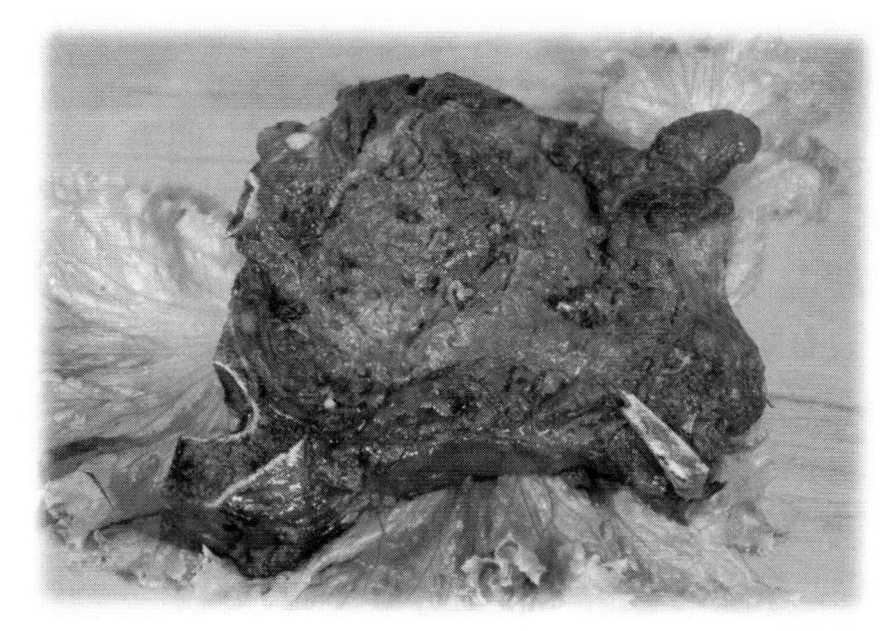

SERVING
4 People

Ingredients

- 2½ pounds boneless beef short ribs, beef brisket, or beef chuck roast cut into 1½- to 2-inch cubes
- 1 tablespoon chili powder
- 1½ teaspoons kosher salt (Diamond Crystal brand)
- 1 tablespoon ghee or fat of choice
- 1 medium onion, thinly sliced
- 1 tablespoon tomato paste
- 6 garlic cloves, peeled and smashed
- ½ cup roasted tomato salsa
- ½ cup bone broth
- ½ teaspoon Red Boat Fish Sauce

Instructions

1. In a large bowl, combine cubed beef, chili powder, and salt.
2. Press the "Sauté" button on your Instant Pot and add the ghee to the cooking insert. Once the fat's melted, add the onions and sauté until translucent. (If you're using a stove top pressure cooker, melt the fat over medium heat and sauté the onions.)
3. Stir in the tomato paste and garlic, and cook for 30 seconds or until fragrant.
4. Toss in the seasoned beef, and pour in the salsa, stock, and fish sauce.
5. Cover and lock the lid, and press the "Keep Warm/Cancel" button on the Instant Pot. Press the "Manual" or "Pressure Cook" button to switch to the pressure cooking mode. Program your IP to cook for 35 minutes under high pressure. If your cubes are smaller than mine, you can press the "minus" button to decrease the cooking time. Once the pot is programmed, walk away. Just cook on high heat until high pressure is reached. Then, reduce the heat to low to maintain high pressure for about 30 minutes.)

- Freshly ground black pepper
- ½ cup minced cilantro (optional)
- 2 radishes, thinly sliced (optional)

6. When the stew is finished cooking, the Instant Pot will switch automatically to a "Keep Warm" mode. If you're using a stove-top pressure cooker instead, remove the pot from the heat. In either case, let the pressure release naturally (~15 minutes).
7. Unlock the lid and season to taste with salt and pepper. At this point, you can plate and serve—or store the beef in the fridge for up to 4 days and reheat right before serving.
8. When you're ready to eat top with cilantro and radishes

Nutrition Information

Calories: 259| Fat: 19g | Carbohydrates: 0g | Fiber: 0 g |Protein: 22 g

Recipe 77: Instant Pot Beef Liver

TIME TO PREPARE
5 minutes

COOK TIME
10 Minutes

SERVING
3 People

Ingredients

- 2 lbs. of beef liver, sliced
- one large onion, sliced
- 2-3 cloves of garlic, diced
- A handful of sliced mushrooms
- 5-6 slices of bacon
- salt and pepper, other herbs or spices to taste

Instructions

1. First, crisp the bacon in an instant pot by sautéing for 2 minutes
2. Once the bacon is cooked most of the way, add the onions and garlic.
3. Then add mushrooms, as well as any other herbs and additional flavorings you might like to taste (like rosemary, parsley, thyme, garlic powder, paprika)
4. Lock the lid of the Instant Pot and cook for about 10 minutes on a high pressure.
5. When the time is up, turn off the Instant Pot
6. Serve and enjoy!

Nutrition Information

Calories: 130| Fat: 3.6g | Carbohydrates: 3.5g | Fiber: 0.0 g |Protein: 19.8g

Recipe 78: Instant Pot Beef Roast

TIME TO PREPARE
6 minutes

COOK TIME
10 Minutes

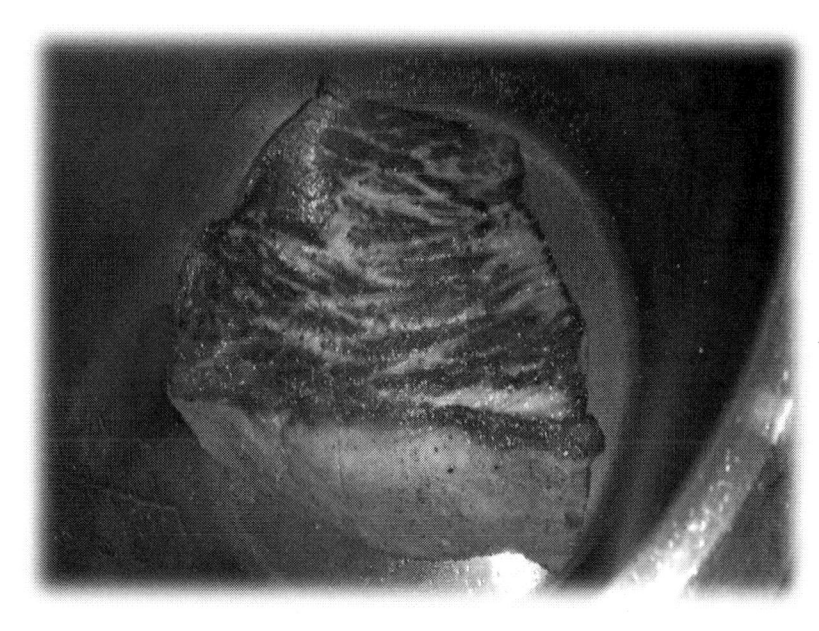

SERVING
4-5 People

Ingredients

- 3-4 lbs chuck or shoulder roast
- 1 Tbsp of EVOO (Extra virgin olive oil)
- 1 1/2 tsp salt or truffle salt
- 1 cup beef broth
- 1/2 cup balsamic vinegar
- 1 Tbsp fish sauce
- 1 Tbsp coconut aminos
- 1 Tbsp honey
- 4 cloves of garlic, crushed
- 1/2 tsp dried lavender or rosemary (or a mix), optional

Instructions

1. Pat the roast dry with paper towels and rub salt on all sides of roast.
2. Add olive oil to Instant Pot and turn it to sauté function.
3. Add roast and sear on all sides (this takes about 2-3 minutes per side).
4. Add remaining ingredients to the Instant Pot.
5. Using pressure cooker function, place lid on the instant pot with Cook on high pressure for 45 minutes
6. Remove roast from Instant Pot, and let rest for 5-10 minutes (you can tent with tinfoil to keep it warm).
7. Meanwhile, reduce the liquid in the instant pot by about two thirds using the sauté function
8. Slice the roast and pour reduction over to serve. Garnish with coarse finishing salt and chopped parsley if desired.
9. Serve and enjoy your dish!

Nutrition Information

Calories: 180| Fat: 6.5g | Carbohydrates: 0.0g | Fiber: 0.0 g |Protein: 28.4g

Recipe 79: Pulled pork

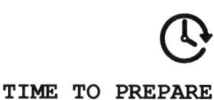

TIME TO PREPARE
8 minutes

COOK TIME
90 Minutes

SERVING
4-5 People

Ingredients

- 4 lb organic bone-in pork shoulder
- 1 tbsp sea salt
- 1 tbsp ground pepper
- 1 tbsp garlic powder
- 1 tbsp onion powder
- 1 tbsp chili powder
- 1 tbsp smoked paprika
- 2 cups chicken stock (or bone broth)
- For the BBQ sauce:
- 1/4 cup tomato paste
- 4-6 dates, soaked for 10-15 minutes in warm water to soften then drained
- 2 tsp garlic powder
- 2 tsp chili powder
- 1/2 cup coconut aminos

Instructions

1. Place all of the seasonings in a small bowl and mix well to make the spice rub.
2. Cut your roast into two pieces if needed to make it more manageable and fit easily. Massage the spice rub all over the meat. You may have some left over if you have a smaller cut of meat.
3. Place the pork into the Instant Pot skin side up and pour the chicken stock in.
4. Cook for 90 minutes on the manual setting, with the vent closed.
5. Once you get the pork in the Instant Pot, make the BBQ sauce. Place all of the sauce ingredients in a blender or food processor and run continuously to combine all the ingredients until smooth. Stop to scrape sides down as needed and restart. Store in fridge until pork is done.
6. Once pork is done, let the pressure release naturally (about 10-15 minutes). Don't do a quick release.
7. Remove the pork from the Instant Pot and place it on a cutting board. Shred with two forks or tongs.

Pour the sauce over the pork and mix it in. Serve and enjoy!

Nutrition Information

Calories: 401| Fat: 22.59g | Carbohydrates: 9.07g | Fiber: 2.2 g |Protein: 38.92g

Recipe 80: Pork with Pineapple

TIME TO PREPARE
10 minutes

COOK TIME
35 Minutes

SERVING
5 People

Ingredients

- 3 pounds of boneless pork shoulder roast
- 2 teaspoons Diamond Crystal brand kosher salt or Magic Mushroom Powder
- 1 tablespoon coconut oil, ghee, or your preferred high temperature cooking fat
- 1 (14-ounce) can pineapple chunks in 100% juice
- 2 Serrano pepper, diced
- 1 tablespoon dried basil
- 1 tablespoon ground cumin
- ½ teaspoon freshly ground black pepper
- 2 tablespoons lime

Instructions

1. Chop the meat into cubes
2. Measure out the Diamond Crystal kosher salt or Magic Mushroom Powder and toss well to coat all the pork pieces.
3. Turn on the Sauté function on your Instant Pot and add the coconut oil once the insert is hot. Toss in the seasoned pork cubes and cook, stirring, until the meat gets a bit of sear on the sides.
4. Drain the pineapple juice and set the pineapple chunks aside
5. You'll be adding ½ cup pineapple juice to the recipe.
6. Turn off the Sauté function on the Instant Pot. Add the diced Serrano peppers, basil, cumin, and black pepper to the pork. Give everything a good stir to distribute the seasoning.
7. Pour in ½ cup pineapple juice and the lime juice. Give everything a good stir.
8. Lock the lid on top and make sure the top valve is pointed to the sealed position
9. Program the Instant Pot to cook under high pressure for 35 minutes, and let the pressure drop

177

- juice
- 2 scallions, thinly sliced

naturally. If you're feeling impatient and hungry, you can manually release the pressure after 20 minutes.
10. Open the lid and check that the pork is fork tender. If the pork is still tough, cook for 5-10 more minutes under high pressure.
11. Stir in the pineapple chunks until warmed through. Taste and adjust for seasoning with additional salt, Magic Mushroom Powder, or lime juice.
12. Ladle up the pork and pineapples and garnish with scallions.

Nutrition Information

Calories: 246.2| Fat: 10g | Carbohydrates: 22.8g | Fiber: 2.4 g |Protein: 18.2g

RECIPE 81: BALSAMIC PORK

TIME TO PREPARE
5 minutes

COOK TIME
20 Minutes

SERVING
3 People

Ingredients

- 1 and 1.5-2 lb pork tenderloin, cut into four pieces
- 1 tbsp of olive oil
- Sauce
- 3 garlic cloves, finely chopped
- 1/4 cup of balsamic vinegar
- 1/4 cup of water
- 1 tbsp of tamari
- 1 tbsp of rosemary, chopped
- 1 tbsp of Almond flour

Instructions

1. Mix all sauce ingredients in a small bowl except almond flour
2. Heat Instant Pot to sauté. Salt and pepper pork pieces and pour 1 tbsp olive oil in the pot.
3. Sauté pork on all sides.
4. Turn off sauté and add sauce to pot. Program Instant Pot to meat and cook for 20 minutes. When the timer beeps, turn pressure cooker off and let the pressure naturally release. Do not skip this step or your meat will be tough.
5. Remove meat from Instant Pot. In a small bowl whisk together almond flour with 2 tbsp water.
6. Add the mixture to the Instant Pot and turn the pot on sauté.
7. Whisk well and let it cook until it thickens a bit.

Nutrition Information

Calories: 257.4| Fat: 9.3g | Carbohydrates: 7.4g | Fiber: 0.0 g |Protein: 33.3g

RECIPE 82: PORK TAGINE

TIME TO PREPARE
4-5 minutes

COOK TIME
20 Minutes

SERVING
3-4 People

Ingredients

- ½ lemon
- ¼ cup tightly packed fresh herbs. I use equal amounts thyme and parsley, and a small stick of rosemary
- 2 tablespoons olive oil
- 1½ pounds pork loin, cut into 5cm / 2 inch cubes
- 1 carrot, peeled and sliced into coins
- 1 stick celery, sliced
- ¼ teaspoon salt
- 3 tablespoons small olives (about 20)
- 1 cup bone broth or water

Instructions

1. Using a good vegetable peeler, remove the zest from the lemon and slice it into small shards. Then, cut away the pith from the flesh. Discard the seeds and the pith.
2. Roughly chop the fresh herbs, and add to the lemon.
3. Pour the olive oil into the Instant Pot and press the 'Sauté' function. Add the pork, celery, carrot and salt. Stir and turn so that the pork pieces brown on all sides. Cancel the 'Sauté' function.
4. Add the lemon, herbs, olives, bone broth or water. Put on the lid and lock it, turning the valve to the 'Sealing' position. Adjust the 'Meat/Stew' function to 'Less': 20 minutes (or 'Manual' for 20 minutes).
5. Go and enjoy your life.
6. When the timer sounds, allow the valve to release

- 1 tablespoon tapioca starch

7. naturally, then remove the lid. Adjust the 'Sauté' function to 'Less' and bring the braising to a slow slimmer.
8. Place the tapioca starch into a small bowl. Add a couple of tablespoons of the braising liquid and add to the starch, stirring to form slurry. Make sure there are no clumps. Add more liquid, stir to combine, and then pour the lot into your mixture. Stir for about a minute until the liquids have thickened.
9. Serve with cauliflower rice or cooked, cold potatoes. And with steam-sautéed vegetables, of course.

Nutrition Information

Calories: 374| Fat: 13.8g | Carbohydrates: 36.5g | Fiber: 6.4 g |Protein: 28.9g

RECIPE 83: INSTANT POT PORK BELLY

TIME TO PREPARE
10 minutes

COOK TIME
50 Minutes

SERVING
4-5 People

Ingredients

- 1 lb of pastured pork belly
- 1 tsp. sea salt
- 1 tsp. smoked paprika
- 1 tsp. thyme
- 4 cloves of garlic (sliced or chopped)
- ½ cup of broth
- ¼ cup sherry (or white wine)
- 2 Tbsp of duck fat

Instructions

1. Rub the fatty side of the pork belly with the salt-spice mixture.
2. Pour the broth and the sherry into the Instant Pot.
3. Now place the pork belly in the instant pot, spice side up.
4. Close and lock the lid. Set the pressure to HIGH and the time to 30 minutes.
5. A few minutes before the time is up, preheat your oven to 400 F. Place a couple tablespoons of duck fat in a cast iron pan. Transfer the pan to the oven to get nice and hot.
6. When the time is up, use two spatulas to lift the cooked pork belly out of the Instant Pot. It will be very tender and may fall apart if you use tongs. Remove any large bits of garlic or spice and place the pork belly fat side down in the preheated cast iron pan.
7. If your pork belly has curled, top it with another cast iron pan to weigh it down. Then pop into the preheated oven for 20 minutes, or to your desired crispness.
8. Allow to cool slightly, and then gently transfer to a cutting board.

9. Using a sharp chef's knife, cut into cubes
10. Sprinkle with a little more sea salt

Nutrition Information

Calories: 259| Fat: 26.5g | Carbohydrates: 0g | Fiber: 0 g |Protein: 4.7g

RECIPE 84: SPINACH STUFFED BEEF ROLLS

TIME TO PREPARE
10 minutes

COOK TIME
35 Minutes

SERVING
5 People

Ingredients

- Butter flied flank steak
- 1 Pinch of Salt and 1 Pinch of ground pepper
- 1Tbsp of olive oil
- 4 Oz of chopped mushrooms
- 1 Minced small shallot
- ¼ Teaspoon of fresh thyme
- 7 Oz of sliced Provolone cheese
- 2 Cups of packed baby spinach

Instructions

1. Slice the steak butter horizontally
2. Pound the meat gently in a meat mallet and season it with pepper and salt; then set it aside.
3. Heat the oil in your Instant Pot; add the mushrooms, the shallots and the thyme.
4. Sprinkle with a little bit of salt and press sauté; then cook for around 5 minutes; then add the spinach and cook for 5 more minutes.
5. Take a baking dish that fits your Instant Pot.
6. Place an aluminium foil in the baking dish and lay the cheese above the beef.
7. Lay the spinach on top and roll the steak up; then tie with a butcher's twine at around 2- inch intervals.
8. Seal the aluminium from its sides and bake place the baking dish in the Instant Pot.
9. Close the lid and set the Instant Pot to high pressure for 25 minutes
10. Once the timer beeps, quick release the pressure.

11. Serve and enjoy your steak roll.

Nutrition Information

Calories: 256.4| Fat: 5.6g | Carbohydrates: 20.5g | Fiber: 0.7 g |Protein: 29.4g

RECIPE 85: PULLED BEEF

TIME TO PREPARE
7 minutes

COOK TIME
50 Minutes

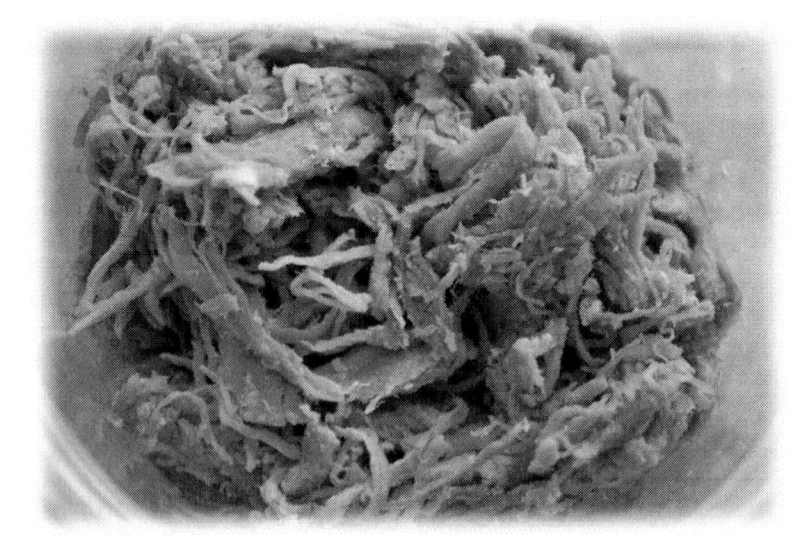

SERVING
5 People

Ingredients

- 3-4 lb of beef rump roast or chuck roast
- 1 tsp sea salt
- 2 tbsp of oil
- 2 1/2 cups of bone broth or beef broth

Instructions

1. Cut the meat into 4 even pieces and season all sides with salt.
2. Set Instant Pot to the Sauté setting and heat the oil in the pot for 10 minutes.
3. Add the roast pieces and brown on all sides, about 10 minutes.
4. Press Cancel, and add the broth over the beef. Close the lid and make sure the pressure-release valve is closed.
5. Cook at high pressure on Manual for 50 minutes. Once the Instant Pot beeps to signal that it's done, let it sit for 10-15 minutes to allow the pressure to release naturally until the lid opens.
6. Transfer the roast to a cutting board, and shred the meat with 2 forks. Return to the Instant Pot and keep warm until ready to use.
7. You can eat the shredded beef on its own with various sides, or use in other dishes like tacos, burrito bowls, stir-fry, sandwiches, and more.

Nutrition Information

Calories: 170.4| Fat: 11g | Carbohydrates: 0.5g | Fiber: 0.1 g |Protein: 16.1g

RECIPE 86: INSTANT POT PORK TENDERLOIN

TIME TO PREPARE
5 minutes

COOK TIME
10 Minutes

SERVING
3 People

Ingredients

- 1.5 - 2 lb. pork tenderloin
- 2 Tbsp. cooking fat
- 2 tsp. salt
- 1 tsp. black pepper
- 1 tsp. oregano
- 1 tsp. thyme
- 1 tsp. paprika
- 1 tsp. garlic, minced
- 1 cup bone broth (chicken or vegetable stock)
- 1/4 cup Primal Kitchen Balsamic Dressing
- 2 Tbsp of honey Mustard Dressing
- 1 Tbsp. coconut aminos
- 1 tsp. arrowroot powder
- 3 tsp. cold cup water

Instructions

1. Season the pork tenderloin with all of the spices. Cut the pork tenderloin in half so that it fits in the Instant Pot.
2. Turn on the Instant Pot to 'Sauté' and add the cooking fat.
3. Once it's hot, add the pork tenderloin. Brown it on all sides for 2 minutes each (4 sides)
4. Add the bone broth, balsamic dressing, and honey mustard and coconut aminos to the pot.
5. Close the lid on the Instant Pot (make sure the pressure valve is closed) and set it to 'Manual' for 6 minutes.
6. Once the Instant Pot beeps that it's down, quick release the pressure and open the lid. Remove the pork tenderloin from the pot, place it on a plate and wrap it in tin-foil to rest.
7. In a small bowl combine the arrowroot powder and water and combine into slurry.
8. Set the Instant Pot to 'Sauté' and add the slurry.
9. Whisk the slurry into the balsamic-honey sauce and bring it to a boil.
10. Once it boils, turn off the Instant Pot and let it sit for 3 minutes to thicken.

11. When you're ready to serve, slice the pork tenderloin and drizzle with balsamic-honey sauce.
12. Serve and enjoy your dish!

Nutrition Information

Calories: 125| Fat: 3.4g | Carbohydrates: 0.0g | Fiber: 0.0 g |Protein: 22g

RECIPE 87: PORK WITH DATES

TIME TO PREPARE
7 minutes

COOK TIME
30 Minutes

SERVING
3-4 People

Ingredients

- 2 lb of pork shoulder or pork neck
- 1 tbsp olive oil
- 1 large onion
- 1 orange
- 1 cup chicken/vegetable stock
- 1 pinch of red chili flakes
- 9 oz baby carrots
- 2 celery sticks
- 10 dried dates
- 1 large handful fresh spinach
- Salt and pepper to taste

Instructions

1. Cut the pork into large 2 inch chunks; then set the Instant Pot to Sauté and when it reads 'Hot' add the oil.
2. Sear the pork until it has a nice golden crust. this will take a few minutes
3. Whilst the pork is browning finely chop the onion.
4. Add the chopped onion to the Instant Pot, stir well then cook for 2 minutes until the onions have started to soften.
5. Add in the stock, the juice of the orange and the chili flakes (if using). Don't add any further seasonings at this stage as the stock has salt in and you won't be able to taste test as you cook.
6. Once the stock and syrup mixture is simmering cancelling Sauté and placing the lid on. Set the Instant Pot to Manual and cook at high pressure for 25 minutes.
7. Whilst the pork stew is cooking prep your veg.
8. Wash and trim the baby carrots (Unless they are really dirty there is no need to peel them)

9. Cut the celery into three chunks and then cut each chunk in half lengthways
10. Chop each dried date into 3 pieces
11. Wash the spinach and set aside
12. When the 25 minutes is up do a Quick Pressure Release.
13. Add in the carrot, celery batons and chopped dates. Close the lid, press Manual and cook on high pressure for a further 5 minutes.
14. Once the time is up do a Quick Pressure Release and stir in the spinach. Then Serve and enjoy your dish!

Nutrition Information

Calories: 204.8| Fat: 5.1g | Carbohydrates: 14.9g | Fiber: 0.1 g |Protein: 24.2g

Recipe 88: Pork with Mushrooms

TIME TO PREPARE
6 minutes

COOK TIME
25 Minutes

SERVING
4-5 People

Ingredients

- 2 pounds of boneless pork roast, trimmed and cut into 1-inch pieces
- 1 medium onion, diced
- 3 tablespoons apple cider vinegar
- 4 to 6 cloves garlic, crushed
- 2 teaspoons grated fresh ginger
- 1 teaspoon honey
- 1 teaspoon ground turmeric
- 1 teaspoon sea salt
- ½ teaspoon ground cilantro
- ½ teaspoon dried basil
- ½ teaspoon dried dill
- ½ teaspoon ground cinnamon

Instructions

1. Place the pork in the Instant Pot steel insert.
2. Add the onion, vinegar, garlic, ginger, honey, turmeric, the salt, the ground cilantro, basil, dill, cinnamon, and ground cloves. Mix well. Cover and place in the refrigerator to marinate for at least two hours.
3. Remove the stainless steel insert from the refrigerator. Place back in the Instant Pot and stir in the broth.
4. Close and lock the lid. Press MANUAL for high pressure.
5. Set cooking time to 15 minutes
6. Once time is up, allow the pressure to release naturally for 10 minutes, then quick release any remaining pressure.
7. Stir in chopped cilantro and serve.

- ⅛ teaspoon ground cloves
- 1 cup bone broth
- ¼ cup chopped fresh cilantro

Nutrition Information

Calories: 580| Fat: 23g | Carbohydrates: 47g | Fiber: 10g |Protein: 50g

CHAPTER 8: TURKEY, GOOSE AND DUCK RECIPES

Recipe 89: Instant Pot Duck Breast

TIME TO PREPARE
5 minutes

COOK TIME
65 Minutes

SERVING
4-6 People

Ingredients

- 4 to 6 duck legs
- 1 pinch of Kosher salt
- 1 Pinch of freshly ground black pepper
- 4 Finely minced or smashed garlic cloves
- 2 Sprigs of thyme, bay leaves, or other type of your favorite herbs

Instructions

1. In a large baking dish, prick the skin of the duck legs in different places
2. Generously season the duck legs on both the sides generously with pepper
3. Place the duck legs with the skin side up on the paper towels in the baking dish; then scatter the garlic and any type of herbs or other of your favorite seasonings and refrigerate for about 24 to 72 hours
4. When you are ready to cook the meat; remove the duck legs from the refrigerator; then heat your Instant Pot by pressing the "sauté" function
5. Sear the duck meat by starting with the skin side down for about 5 to 8 minutes
6. Arrange the duck legs in the bottom of your Instant Pot; then add in the garlic cloves and the herbs or the spices and make sure to scrape any fats from the bottom of the Instant Pot
7. Cover your Instant Pot; then seal the valve and cook on High for about 60 minutes
8. Serve and enjoy your dish!

Nutrition Information

Calories: 205| Fat: 11g | Carbohydrates: 1g| Fiber: 0g |Protein: 25g

Recipe 90: Middle Eastern-Style Turkey

TIME TO PREPARE
10 minutes

COOK TIME
40 Minutes

SERVING
2 People

Ingredients

- 1 Turkey Leg
- 250 ml or White Rice
- 1 Tbsp of Garlic Puree
- 2 Tbsp of Olive Oil
- 250 ml of Turkey Stock
- 2 Tbsp of Honey
- 2 Tbsp of Oregano
- 2 Tbsp of Thyme
- 1 Pinch of salt
- 1 Pinch of pepper

Instructions

1. In a large mixing bowl; combine all together the thyme with the oregano, the honey, the garlic, the salt and the pepper.
2. Massage the olive oil into the skin of the turkey and massage with the marinade very well
3. Place your Instant Pot on the setting sauté and add in the turkey and sauté for about 3 minutes
4. Turn the turkey meat over so that its skin faces up; then pour the stock over and change the setting of the instant Pot to the setting "poultry"; then set to sealing and cook for about 40 minutes
5. When the 40 minutes are finished up, remove the turkey meat; then let rest over a clean chopping board
6. Rinse your rice under cold water; then place the rice after draining it very well on the bottom of your Instant Pot with the same amount of water and cook for about 3 minutes on the rice setting and let cool down; then don't release the pressure after 10 minutes
7. Remove the rice from the Instant Pot and place the turkey on top
8. Serve and enjoy your dish!

Nutrition Information

Calories: 289.6| Fat: 10.1g | Carbohydrates: 33.1g| Fiber: 2.4g |Protein: 18.1g

RECIPE 91: ORANGE TURKEY

TIME TO PREPARE
10 minutes

COOK TIME
40 Minutes

SERVING
2 People

Ingredients

- 3 Large Oranges
- ½ Pound of Turkey Breasts
- 1 Chopped, spring Onion
- 2 Tablespoons of Honey
- 1 Tablespoon of Thyme
- 1 Tablespoon of Basil
- 1 Teaspoon of Paprika
- 1 Teaspoon of Celery Salt
- 1 Pinch of salt
- 1 Pinch of pepper

Instructions

1. Start by making the marinade and to do that, grate the oranges and put the zest on a side; then add the juice and the oranges into a mixing bowl
2. Add the seasonings to a bowl; then add the honey and mix very well
3. Clean and chop the spring onion; then put it to a side
4. Chop the turkey breasts; then place it in a mixing bowl with the marinade; then mix very well and cover with a silver foil
5. Place in your refrigerator for 1 hour; then lay the silver foil in a way that you have the turkey breast into foil packet
6. In your Instant Pot; add the cup of water and place the steam shelf on top
7. Place the silver foil packet over; then set it to the function poultry and pressure cook for about 8 minutes; then let rest for 2 minutes and manually release the pressure and remove the turkey to a dinner plate
8. Pour over the fresh spring onion with the orange rind; then serve and enjoy your dish!

Nutrition Information

Calories: 144| Fat: 1g | Carbohydrates: 20g| Fiber: 2. g |Protein: 14g

Recipe 92: Stuffed Turkey breast

TIME TO PREPARE
15 minutes

COOK TIME
60 Minutes

SERVING
5 People

Ingredients

- 2 tbsp of butter
- 1 medium finely minced shallot
- 1 medium peeled and finely minced garlic clove
- 4 ounces of bulk sweet Italian sausage meat
- 1/4 cup of chopped raisins
- 1 cup of fresh breadcrumbs
- 1 tsp of finely grated lemon zest
- 1/2 tsp of fennel seeds
- 2 and 1/2 lbs of butterflied boneless and skinless turkey breast, opened up
- 1/2 tsp of table salt
- 1/2 tsp of ground black pepper

Instructions

1. Press the setting Sauté of your Instant Pot and set the timer for about 10 minutes
2. Melt about 1 tablespoon of butter in your Instant Pot and add the garlic and the shallot; then cook for about 2 minutes
3. Add in the sausage meat and cook while stirring for about 4 minutes; then turn off the sauté function and scrape the contents of the pot's insert in a large bowl; then cool for about 4 minutes
4. Let cool for about 5 minutes; then add in the raisins, the
5. breadcrumbs, the lemon zest and the fennel seeds; then cool for about 10 minutes
6. Place the turkey breast with the split side up over a large cutting board
7. Spread the mixture of the breadcrumb in an even layer on top of the meat; then roll the meat up from the long edge in a way that you form a spiraled log
8. Tie the log into three places with a butchers' twine; then season with salt and pepper
9. Press the setting sauté and set the timer for about 10 minutes
10. Melt in the remaining quantity of butter; then add in the stuffed turkey and brown on all sides lightly

- 1 1/2 cups of chicken broth
- 2 fresh oregano sprigs
- 1 1/2 tbsp of Water
- 1 tbsp of cornstarch

turning from time to time for about 4 to 5 minutes.

11. Turn off the function SAUTÉ; then pour in the broth and tuck the sprigs of oregano around the meat and close the lid of your Instant Pot on it
12. Press the pressure cooker on Max pressure cooker for about 25 minutes; make sure the Keep Warm setting is off
13. Press the Meat/Stew or the Pressure cook (Manual) on a High pressure for about 35 minutes
14. When the pressure cooking cycle is finished; turn off your Instant pot and let the pressure come to normal naturally for about 25 minutes.
15. Unlock the lid of your Instant pot; then find the oregano sprigs and discard it
16. Transfer the turkey roll to a cutting board
17. Press the setting sauté for about; then let the sauce simmer and whisk the water with the cornstarch in a bowl and mix until it becomes smooth
18. Whisk the slurry or cornstarch into the sauce; then keep whisking for about 1 to 2 minutes
19. Immediately turn off the sauté function and remove the insert from the Instant Pot to stop the cooking process
20. Slice the stuffed turkey breast into slices of 1 inch of thickness
21. Serve and enjoy your dish with the sauce!

Nutrition Information

Calories: 241.9| Fat: 2.6g | Carbohydrates: 4.4g| Fiber: 1.1g |Protein: 49.1g

RECIPE 93: TURKEY MEATBALLS WITH TOMATO SAUCE

TIME TO PREPARE
8 minutes

COOK TIME
9 Minutes

SERVING
7 People

Ingredients

- 1 lb of ground turkey
- 1 large egg
- ¼ Cup of oats
- 2 grated large garlic cloves
- 2 tbsp of onion flakes
- 1 Small grated onion
- 1/2 tbsp of balsamic vinegar
- ½ tsp of dried oregano
- ½ tsp of salt
- 1 Pinch of Ground black pepper, to taste
- 1 Can of 15 oz of low sodium tomato sauce

Instructions

1. Pour ½ cup of water to your Instant Pot; then place a trivet or steamer basket inside and set aside
2. Add a can of tomato sauce with no water; then set aside
3. In a large bowl; add the ground meat, the grated onion, the garlic, the oregano, the salt and the pepper.
4. Mix your ingredients very well with your hand or with a spatula
5. Form 30 meatballs with a scoop and place them one by one in your Instant Pot in one layer in the tomato sauce
6. Close the lid of your Instant Pot; and turn the pressure release valve to a Sealing position and pressure cook for about 7 minutes
7. Wait For about 2 minutes; then release any remaining pressure with the quick release method
8. Open the lid of your Instant Pot; then serve and enjoy your dish!

Nutrition Information

Calories: 118| Fat: 5.8g | Carbohydrates: 1.3g| Fiber: 0.2g |Protein: 15g

RECIPE 94: TURKEY MEATLOAF

TIME TO PREPARE
7 minutes

COOK TIME
30 Minutes

SERVING
6 People

Ingredients

- 8 oz of Ground Turkey Meat
- 2 Tablespoons of Ketchup
- ¼ Cup of chopped onion
- ¼ Cup of Bread Crumbs
- ½ Cup of cubed Red Potatoes
- Fresh chopped cauliflower
- 1 Tablespoon of minced garlic
- 2 Tablespoon of Butter
- 1 Large egg
- 1 Pinch of salt and 1 pinch of Pepper
- 2 Teaspoons of Worcestershire Sauce
- 1 Teaspoon of Thyme

Instructions

1. Place the rack in your Instant Pot and pour in the water in it
2. Chop the garlic and the onion in a bowl with the bread crumbs, the egg, and the spices.
3. Cut off a piece of aluminum foil; then place over your counter
4. Take the turkey meat and place on the aluminum foil; then fold up the edges
5. Drizzle the ketchup over the top of the meatloaf and cover the top
6. Put the turkey meatloaf in your Instant Pot and turn it on; the press the "Pressure cook" And pressure cook for about 30 minutes
7. In the meantime, prepare the potatoes and the cauliflower
8. Place the ingredients on a piece of aluminum foil; then add the butter and the seasoning
9. Once your Instant Pot beeps; click the cancel button, and apply a Quick Release.
10. Add in the potatoes and the cauliflower on the top of the meatloaf and close the lid; then click "pressure cook" for about 5 minutes
11. Once perfectly done, remove the meatloaf from the

- 1 Teaspoon of chopped Parsley
- 1 Cup of water
- Aluminum Foil

Instant Pot; then serve and enjoy your dish!

Nutrition Information

Calories: 240| Fat: 8g | Carbohydrates: 32g| Fiber: 5g |Protein: 14g

Recipe 95: Turkey Chili

TIME TO PREPARE
6 minutes

COOK TIME
25 Minutes

SERVING
3-4 People

Ingredients

- 2 tablespoons of olive oil
- 1 pound of ground turkey
- 1 medium finely chopped onion
- 1 Medium, cored and finely diced green bell pepper
- 3 Medium, peeled and thinly sliced carrot
- 3 Thinly sliced celery stalks
- 3 Finely minced garlic cloves
- 1 Can of 28 ounces of crushed tomatoes
- 1 Can of drained and rinsed 15 ounces of black beans

Instructions

1. Place the oil in your electric pressure cooker, Instant Pot. Turn on the sauté function and heat the oil until it starts shimmering
2. Add in the turkey and cook for about 4 minutes or until the meat starts breaking up into small pieces
3. Add in the onion, the bell pepper, the carrots, the celery, and the garlic and cook for about 3 minutes
4. Add in the tomatoes; the black beans; the green chiles, the water; the chili powder, the cumin, the salt and the tamari or soy sauce
5. Stir very well to combine your ingredients; then secure the lid and close its vent. Set the cooking time for about 20 minutes at High pressure and when the cooking time ends up; open the valve to quick release the pressure; then open the lid when it is safe to do it
6. Stir your chili; then adjust the taste of salt or soy sauce
7. Serve and enjoy your chili with toppings of your choice!

- 1 Can of about 4 ounces of finely drained chopped green chiles
- ½ cup of water
- 3 tablespoons of chili powder
- 1 ½ teaspoons of ground cumin
- 1 teaspoon of kosher salt
- 1 teaspoon of tamari or of soy sauce
- For the toppings for serving: shredded cheddar cheese
- Sliced scallions
- Chopped
- Sour cream

Nutrition Information

Calories: 224| Fat: 7.75g | Carbohydrates: 19.68g| Fiber: 6.1g |Protein: 19.75g

RECIPE 96: CURRIED GROUND TURKEY

TIME TO PREPARE
8 minutes

COOK TIME
23 Minutes

SERVING
4 People

Ingredients

- 3 to 4 Tbsp of vegetable oil
- 1 pound of ground turkey
- 1 Finely chopped onion
- 1 to 2 finely chopped fresh red chiles
- 1 Pinch of salt
- 1 Piece of 1 inch of peeled grated ginger
- 2 Finely minced garlic cloves
- 1 Tablespoon of Garam Masala
- 1 teaspoon of turmeric
- 1 teaspoon of ground cumin
- 1 teaspoon of ground coriander
- 1/2 cup of water
- 2 large, peeled and

Instructions

1. Start by browning the ground turkey; then heat the vegetable oil in your Instant Pot by pressing the setting sauté
2. When the oil heats up; add in the ground turkey and spread over the pan
3. Sauté for about 4 to 5 minutes; then add in the onion and the chilies
4. Sprinkle with the salt; then add in the ginger and the garlic and mix very well; then sauté for about 1 to 2 additional minutes
5. Add in the spices, the water, the potatoes and close the lid of the Instant Pot, then turn the valve to sealing position
6. Set the timer to about 20 minutes
7. When the pressure cooking time is up, quick release the pressure; then open the lid when it is safe to do it
8. Add in the tomatoes and the peas and press the function sauté; then cook for about 3 additional minutes
9. Add in the salt if needed; then stir in the chopped cilantro
10. Mix in the chopped cilantro; then serve and enjoy your dish with flat bread!

- chopped Yukon Gold potatoes
- 2 to 4 chopped Roma or plum tomatoes
- 1 Cup of fresh or frozen peas
- 1/2 cup of chopped parsley

Nutrition Information

Calories: 244.8| Fat: 7.6g | Carbohydrates: 19.7g| Fiber: 2g |Protein: 24.2g

Recipe 97: Ground Turkey with Peppers

TIME TO PREPARE
5 minutes

COOK TIME
10 Minutes

SERVING
3 People

Ingredients

- 3 to 4 tablespoons of extra virgin olive oil
- 1 cup of chopped yellow onion
- 1 Chopped red or yellow bell pepper
- 2 Minced garlic cloves
- 1 Pinch of kosher salt
- 1 pound of ground turkey thighs
- 1 teaspoon of chipotle powder or of chili powder
- 2 tablespoons of chopped fresh parsley or chopped cilantro

Instructions

1. Start your Instant Pot by pressing the setting sauté; then heat in 2 tablespoons of olive oil; then add in the onions, the bell pepper and the garlic and cook for 2 minutes
2. Add in the chopped onions and the bell pepper and sauté for about 2 to 3 minutes
3. Add in the garlic cook for about 1 to 2 minutes
4. Add in the ground turkey, the salt and the chipotle chili powder
5. Add in one or 2 additional tablespoons of oil; then add in the ground turkey and sprinkle with 1 pinch of salt and with the chili powder
6. Sauté the turkey for about 2 to 3 minutes; then stir in the peppers and the onions and the peppers and sprinkle with salt and chili powders
7. Remove from the heat; then stir in the fresh chopped parsley or the cilantro
8. Serve and enjoy your dish!

Nutrition Information

Calories: 177| Fat: 5.1g | Carbohydrates: 22.2g| Fiber: 3.3g |Protein: 13.2g

Recipe 98: Turkey Burgers

TIME TO PREPARE
6 minutes

COOK TIME
7 Minutes

SERVING
4 People

Ingredients

- 1 lightly beaten egg
- 2 tablespoons of finely chopped onion
- 2 tablespoons of chopped fresh parsley
- 2 Finely minced garlic cloves
- 2 teaspoons of Worcestershire sauce optional
- ½ teaspoon of salt
- ¼ teaspoon of pepper
- 1 Pound of ground turkey
- olive oil or other type of vegetable oil for cooking

For Serving:

- Lettuce
- burger buns

Instructions

1. Place the egg, the onion, the parsley, the garlic, the Worcestershire sauce, the salt and the pepper in a large bowl.
2. Mix your ingredients with a fork to combine very well; then add in the ground turkey
3. Divide the mixture of the turkey into 4 equal parts and shape into patties that are about 1/2-inch of thickness
4. Start your Instant Pot by pressing the setting sauté
5. Heat about 1 to 2 tablespoons of oil in your Instant pot
6. Add in the turkey patties; then sauté for about 3 to 4 minutes per side
7. Serve and enjoy your turkey burgers!

- Sliced red onion
- Avocado, ketchup or guacamole
- Mustard and BBQ sauce as desired

Nutrition Information

Calories: 150| Fat: 5g | Carbohydrates: 2g| Fiber: 2g |Protein: 22g

Recipe 99: Quinoa Bowl

TIME TO PREPARE
6 minutes

COOK TIME
7 Minutes

SERVING
4 People

Ingredients

- 1 lb of ground turkey
- 1 tbsp of oil
- 1 tsp of taco seasoning, low sodium
- 1 tsp of dried oregano
- 1 tsp of salt
- 1 pinch of ground black pepper
- 1 ½ cups of water
- 1 and ½ cups of uncooked quinoa
- 1 large, finely chopped onion
- 3 grated garlic cloves
- 1 Finely chopped bell pepper
- 2 tbsp of soy sauce
- 2 tbsp of maple syrup or honey
- 2 cups of frozen green peas
- 2 cups of frozen corn

Instructions

1. Press the setting sauté; then wait until you see the display Hot; it would usually take about 3 to 5 minutes
2. Swirl the oil to coat; then add in the ground turkey and cook for about 5 minutes; then add in the taco seasoning, the oregano, the salt, the pepper and the water and stir to deglaze the bottom of the Instant Pot
3. Press the button "Cancel"; then add the quinoa and stir
4. Add in the onion, the garlic, the bell pepper, the soy sauce and the maple syrup; but don't stir this time and move the pressure valve to Sealing position and cook on Low for about 12 minutes
5. Do a quick release pressure; and turn the valve to venting position
6. Add in the peas and the corn and stir; then close he lid and pressure cook on Low for about 12 minutes
7. Release the pressure using the Quick release method; then turn the valve to Venting
8. Add the peas and the corn and close the lid; then let the quinoa rest for 5 minutes
9. Add the green onions; then serve and enjoy your

- 1/4 Cup of finely chopped green onion

dish!

Nutrition Information

Calories: 256.1| Fat: 7.2g | Carbohydrates: 45.7g| Fiber: 8.5g |Protein: 9.5g

CHAPTER 9: STOCKS AND SAUCES RECIPES

Recipe 100: Spaghetti Sauce

TIME TO PREPARE
5 minutes

COOK TIME
10 Minutes

SERVING
4 People

Ingredients

- 1 lb of ground Italian sausage
- 1 medium, finely diced yellow onion
- 1 Cup of beef broth
- 1 Can of 28 oz of crushed tomatoes
- 1 can of 14.5 oz of diced tomatoes
- 2 Tbsp of tomato paste
- 1 to 2 bay leaves
- 2 tsp of dried basil
- 1 tsp of garlic powder
- ½ tsp of dried oregano
- 1 tsp of brown sugar
- 1 Pinch of salt and 1 pinch of pepper

Instructions

1.
2. Turn the Instant Pot to the function sauté and when you see the Display HOT, add the sausage
3. With a wooden spoon, break up the sausage and sauté for about 5 minutes
4. Add the onion and sauté for about 3 minutes
5. Deglaze the pot with the broth; then add in the tomatoes, the chopped tomatoes, the tomato paste, the bay leaf, the basil, the garlic powder, the oregano and the brown sugar
6. Cover your Instant Pot and secure the lid; then make sure the valve is in sealing position
7. Set the Manual of the pressure cooker to about 10 minutes on High pressure and when the time is up; naturally release the pressure for about 10 minutes and move the valve to venting position
8. Remove the lid of the Instant Pot and stir your sauce; then discard the bay leaf, the salt and the pepper
9. Serve and enjoy with the pasta!

Nutrition Information

Calories: 145| Fat: 9g | Carbohydrates: 8g| Fiber: 1g |Protein: 7g

Recipe 101: Chicken Stock

TIME TO PREPARE
6 minutes

COOK TIME
40 Minutes

SERVING
3-4 People

Ingredients

- The leftover chicken from 1 whole roasted chicken rotisserie
- 1 large, finely chopped onion
- 1 ginger
- A few springs of fresh thyme
- 2 to 3 bay leaves
- 1 large finely chopped carrot
- 1 Celery stalk
- 1 Pinch of salt to taste
- A small Bunch of fresh parsley
- 1 Garlic bulb
- 3 litres of water

Instructions

1. Chop the onion, the carrot; the celery stalk, the ginger and the garlic bulb into the halves.
2. Put the chicken bones, the thyme, the bay leaves, the parsley and the rest of the ingredients in the inner pot of your Instant Pot
3. Add the salt and the black pepper; then cover with about 3 litres of water
4. Lock the lid of the Instant Pot and turn the valve to sealing position
5. Select the manual on HIGH pressure and set the timer for about 40 minutes
6. Leave to cool; then skim off any fats and remove the bones and any other vegetables; then strain the stock through a sieve or a muslin cloth
7. Divide into portions; then store the stock into jars or in a container!

Nutrition Information

Calories: 86| Fat: 2.9g | Carbohydrates: 8.5g| Fiber: 0.0g |Protein: 6g

Recipe 102: Bolognese sauce

TIME TO PREPARE
5 minutes

COOK TIME
20 Minutes

SERVING
3 People

Ingredients

- 4 ounces of pancetta, or center chopped bacon
- 1 tablespoon of unsalted butter
- 1 large, finely minced white onion
- 2 Minced celery stalks
- 2 Finely minced carrots
- 2 lb of lean ground beef
- ¼ cup of dry white wine
- 2 cans of about 28 oz of crushed tomatoes
- 2 to 3 bay leaves
- ½ teaspoon of kosher salt
- ½ Pinch of fresh black pepper

Instructions

1. Press the setting function sauté on your Instant Pot, sauté the pancetta over a low heat for about 4 to 5 minutes
2. Add in the butter, the onion, the celery and the carrots and cook for about 6 to 8 minutes
3. Add in the meat and season with about ¾ teaspoons of salt and the black pepper and sauté for about 4 to 5 minutes, making sure to break the meat into small pieces
4. Add in the wine and cook for about 3 to 4 minutes; then add in the crushed tomatoes, the bay leaves, ¾ teaspoon of salt and the fresh black pepper; then cover and cook on high pressure for about 15 minutes
5. Naturally release the pressure; then add in the half & half and garnish with the parsley
6. Serve over your favorite pasta and enjoy!

- ½ cup of half & half cream
- ¼ cup of chopped fresh parsley

Nutrition Information

Calories: 191| Fat: 8.5g | Carbohydrates: 12.5g| Fiber: 1g |Protein: 12g

Recipe 103: Cream Béchamel

TIME TO PREPARE
5 minutes

COOK TIME
5 Minutes

SERVING
3 People

Ingredients

- 1 Cup of butter
- 1 Cup of flour
- ½ l of milk
- 1 Pinch of salt
- 1 Pinch of pepper
- Nutmeg

Instructions

1. Set your instant pot in the mode browning, sauté
2. Add in the butter and once the butter melts, add in the flour and stir
3. Add the salt, the pepper and the spice and mix until the cream becomes thick
4. Pour the béchamel sauce over spaghetti or pasta; then serve and enjoy!

Nutrition Information

Calories: 399.3| Fat: 23.2g | Carbohydrates: 39.4g| Fiber: 0.9g |Protein: 11.6g

Recipe 104: Mornay Sauce

TIME TO PREPARE
6 minutes

COOK TIME
5 Minutes

SERVING
3 People

Ingredients

- 2 ½ Tbsp of unsalted butter
- 3 Tbsp of all-purpose flour
- 2 cups of whole milk, warmed
- ¼ tsp of salt
- 1/8 tsp of white pepper
- 2 oz of grated Gruyere cheese

Instructions

1. Melt the butter in a medium Instant Pot over a medium-high heat by pressing the setting sauté
2. Once the Display HOT shows up; melted, whisk in the flour to make a roux; then keep whisking until the roux becomes pale and frothy
3. Slowly add in the milk and cook while whisking for about 2 minutes
4. Add in the salt and the pepper and sauté for about 2 to 3 minutes
5. Add in the cheese and whisk until perfectly melted
6. Serve and enjoy your Stir in cheese and whisk until it is completely melted.
7. Serve immediately and enjoy!

Nutrition Information

Calories: 110| Fat: 7.9g | Carbohydrates: 39.4g| Fiber: 0.2g |Protein: 4.4g

Recipe 105: Mushroom Sauce

TIME TO PREPARE
4 minutes

COOK TIME
6 Minutes

SERVING
3 People

Ingredients

- 1 and ½ cups of sliced shiitake mushroom caps
- 1 Tablespoon of all-purpose flour
- 1/3 cup of port or other sweet red wine
- ¼ cup of minced shallots
- 1 tablespoon of balsamic vinegar
- 1 cup of beef broth
- 2 teaspoons of Worcestershire sauce
- 1 teaspoon of tomato paste
- 1/8 teaspoon of dried rosemary
- ½ teaspoon of Dijon mustard

Instructions

1. Combine the mushrooms and the flour in a bowl and toss very well.
2. Combine the wine, the shallots, and the vinegar in your Instant Pot and press the setting sauté.
3. Sauté for about 3 minutes; then add the broth, the Worcestershire, the tomato paste, and the rosemary and cook for about 1 minute.
4. Add in the mushroom mixture and cook for about 3 minutes while stirring
5. Add in the mustard
6. Serve and enjoy!

Nutrition Information

Calories: 279| Fat: 23g | Carbohydrates: 15g| Fiber: 1.5g |Protein: 5.8g

Recipe 106: Custard Sauce

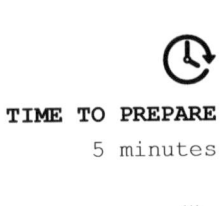

TIME TO PREPARE
5 minutes

COOK TIME
7 Minutes

SERVING
3-4 People

Ingredients

- 3 Lightly beaten eggs
- ⅓ Cup of sugar
- 2 Cups of milk
- ¼ teaspoon of ground nutmeg

Instructions

1. In a mixing bowl, combine the eggs with the sugar, the vanilla, and the milk and mix very well.
2. Pour the mixture in an Instant Pot and sprayed with nonstick-cooking spray
3. Sprinkle with nutmeg; then pour in 1 and ½ cups of water to the inner pot and place a trivet in your Instant Pot
4. Close the lid of your Instant Pot and turn the vale to sealing position
5. Cook on High for about 7 minutes and when the time is up; do a quick release pressure method
6. Top with your favorite toppings like caramel and enjoy!

Nutrition Information

Calories: 186| Fat: 7g | Carbohydrates: 22g| Fiber: 3g |Protein: 7g

Recipe 107: Chocolate Sauce

TIME TO PREPARE
5 minutes

COOK TIME
5 Minutes

SERVING
2-3 People

Ingredients

- 1.25 cups of White Sugar
- ½ cup of Heavy Cream Half & Half or of Whole Milk
- 4 Tablespoons of Butter
- ¼ cup of Dutch Processed Cocoa
- ¼ cup of Natural Cocoa Powder
- 1 Pinch of sea salt
- 1 teaspoon of Pure Vanilla Extract

Instructions

1. Combine the sugar, the milk, the butter, the cocoa and the salt in an Instant Pot by pressing the setting sauté
2. Let boil for about 3 to 5 minutes while whisking constantly
3. Remove the sauce from the heat; then stir in the vanilla
4. Let cool; then serve and enjoy while still warm!

Nutrition Information

Calories: 184| Fat: 9g | Carbohydrates: 27g| Fiber: 1g |Protein: 1g

RECIPE 108: MEXICAN-STYLE BARBECUE SAUCE

TIME TO PREPARE
6 minutes

COOK TIME
15 Minutes

SERVING
3 People

Ingredients

- 2 Finely chopped onions
- 3 tbsp of oil
- 2 cups of ketchup
- 6 Finely minced garlic cloves
- 2 tbsp of chili powder
- ½ Cup of apple cider vinegar
- ½ Cup of brown sugar
- 4 tbsp of Worcestershire sauce
- 1 tsp of salt
- ½ tsp of black pepper

Instructions

1. Add the oil and the onions to the Instant Pot and press the setting function "Sauté"
2. Set the timer to about 15 minutes and sauté the onions while stirring every 30 seconds
3. Press the "cancel" button to stop sautéing; then add the Ketchup, the garlic, the chili powder, the apple cider vinegar, the brown sugar, the Worcestershire sauce, the salt and the pepper
4. Close the Instant Pot and turn the valve to sealing position; then press the "Pressure Cook" button and set the timer to about 5 minutes on High pressure
5. When the pressure cooking cycle is done, let the pressure naturally release for about 5 minutes; then do a quick release method to release any remaining steam
6. Store the sauce in the refrigerator!

Nutrition Information

Calories: 131| Fat: 4g | Carbohydrates: 24g| Fiber: 1g |Protein: 1g

Recipe 109: Mexican-Style Barbecue Sauce

TIME TO PREPARE
6 minutes

COOK TIME
15 Minutes

SERVING
3 People

Ingredients

- ¼ Cup of butter
- 1 teaspoon of salt
- 1 teaspoon of ground black pepper
- 1 teaspoon of onion powder
- 2 tablespoons of tapioca starch
- 1 and ¼ cups of whole milk
- 1 and ½ cups of grated sharp Cheddar cheese

Instructions

1. Turn on your Instant Pot by pressing the setting sauté; then add in the butter and let melt
2. Season with the salt, the pepper and the onion powder and stir
3. Sprinkle with the tapioca starch and stir the roux until it is blended
4. Pour in the milk gradually by pouring ¼ cup at a time and stir with each addition and keep stirring to remove any clumps
5. Turn off your Instant Pot and set to Keep Warm
6. Add in the Cheddar cheese and stir continuously until the cheese melts
7. Serve and enjoy your sauce!

Nutrition Information

Calories: 223| Fat: 5.4g | Carbohydrates: 8.8g| Fiber: 1g |Protein: 1g

Recipe 110: Espagnole Sauce

TIME TO PREPARE
3 minutes

COOK TIME
10 Minutes

SERVING
3 People

Ingredients

- 1 cup of white sugar
- 1 cup of orange juice
- 1 package of about 12 ounces of fresh cranberries

Instructions

1. Press the setting sauté of your Instant Pot and add in the sugar and the orange juice
2. Stir in the cranberries and close the lid of your Instant Pot
3. Press the Cancel button to cancel the sauté function and seal the valve to sealed position
4. Set the timer for about 10 minutes at High pressure
5. Turn off your Instant Pot; then quick release the pressure and open the valve when it is safe to do it
   Transfer the cranberry sauce to a bowl
   Serve and enjoy!

Nutrition Information

Calories: 110| Fat: 0g | Carbohydrates: 25g| Fiber: 1g |Protein: 0g

Calories: 110| Fat: 0g | Carbohydrates: 25g| Fiber: 1g |Protein: 0g

Recipe 111: Enchilada Sauce

TIME TO PREPARE
5 minutes

COOK TIME
10 Minutes

SERVING
3-4 People

Ingredients

- ½ Red, finely chopped onion
- ½ Green, finely chopped bell pepper
- ½ Finely sliced Jalapeño pepper
- 4 Garlic cloves
- 2 Chipotle Chile in Adobo Sauce
- 1 teaspoon of Ground Cumin
- 1 to 2 teaspoons of Mexican Red Chili Powder
- 1 to 2 teaspoons of salt
- ½ cup of water
- 14 ounces of canned Fire Roasted Tomatoes

Instructions

1. Put all your ingredients in the Instant Pot, except for the tomatoes and stir very well.
2. Pour the tomatoes over the top and do not over mix.
3. Close the lid of your Instant Pot and cook on High Pressure for about 10 minutes, letting the pressure naturally release
4. With an immersion blender, purée the sauce and wait for a few seconds until it cools down
5. Use the sauce and enjoy it!

Nutrition Information

Calories: 79| Fat: 1g | Carbohydrates: 16g| Fiber: 3g |Protein: 3g

Recipe 112: Bordelaise Sauce

TIME TO PREPARE
10 minutes

COOK TIME
25 Minutes

SERVING
4 People

Ingredients

- 1 cup of Demi-Glace store bought Glace
- 1 and ¼ cups of red wine
- 1 to 2 thyme sprig
- 1 to 2 Bay leaves
- 2 tablespoons of minced shallots
- 2 ounces of marrow from ½ to 1 pound of beef bones
- 1 Can of 15 ounces of low sodium beef broth
- 1 Pinch of freshly ground black pepper

Instructions

1. In a medium pot, add the wine, the thyme, the bay leaf and the shallots
2. Simmer for about 5 minutes
3. With the end of a small spoon, push the marrows out of the bones; and transfer to your Instant Pot
4. Pour in the beef broth to the marrow and cover your Instant Pot with the lid
5. Set the timer to about 7 to 10 minutes at High Pressure when the pressure cooking cycle is over, turn off your Instant Pot and do a quick release pressure
6. Open the lid of the Instant Pot when it is safe to do and transfer to a cutting board
7. Mince the meat marrow and set it aside.
8. Add the demi-glace and the ground of fresh pepper to the Instant Pot and lock the lid; then set the timer for about 10 minutes at High pressure
9. When the timer beeps; do a quick release pressure; then stain the sauce through a fine mesh strainer; then add in the diced bone marrow
10. Serve and enjoy!

Nutrition Information

Calories: 128| Fat: 2g | Carbohydrates: 9g| Fiber: 2g |Protein: 9g

RECIPE 113: SPICY INDIAN SAUCE

TIME TO PREPARE
7 minutes

COOK TIME
15 Minutes

SERVING
3 People

Ingredients

- 2 tablespoons of extra virgin olive oil
- 3 Finely diced large onions
- 3 Finely chopped garlic cloves
- 1 Inch of peeled and grated and knob fresh ginger
- ¾ teaspoon of fine grain sea salt, plus more to taste
- 1 tablespoon of ground coriander
- 1 tablespoon of ground cumin
- ¾ teaspoon of cayenne pepper
- 1 teaspoon of ground turmeric
- 1 tablespoon of sweet

Instructions

1. Press the setting Sauté setting on your Instant Pot and heat the oil in it
2. Add in the onions, the garlic, the ginger, the salt and sauté for about 10 minutes
3. Add in the coriander, the cumin, the cayenne, the turmeric, the paprika, and the garam masala
4. Add in the tomatoes and the liquid, crushing and breaking up the tomatoes as you add to the Instant Pot
5. Pour in the water and secure the lid of your Instant Pot
6. Make sure the valve is in sealing position and press the button CANCEL; then press MANUAL for about 15 minutes at high pressure; then naturally release for about 10 minutes; then quickly release any remaining pressure
7. Serve and enjoy the sauce!

- paprika
- 1 tablespoon of garam masala
- 1 can of 28 ounces of whole tomatoes with the liquid
- 1 cup of water

Nutrition Information

Calories: 268| Fat: 19g | Carbohydrates: 21g| Fiber: 4.5g |Protein: 4.2g

Recipe 114: Sweet red Chili Sauce

TIME TO PREPARE
5 minutes

COOK TIME
20 Minutes

SERVING
3 People

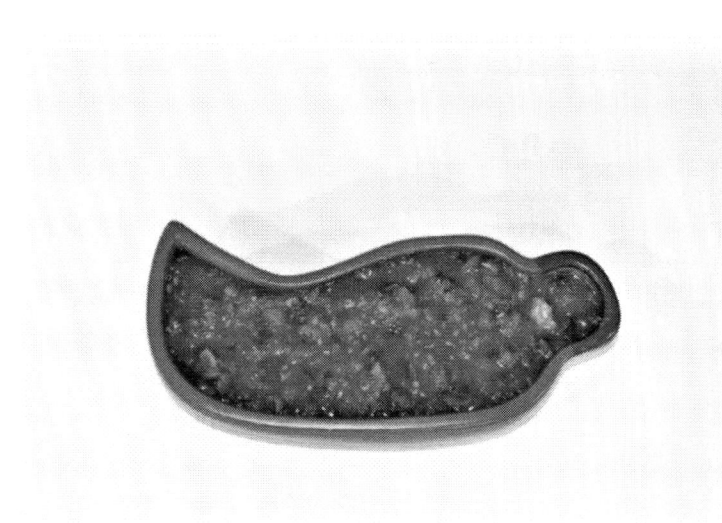

Ingredients

- 2 Halved and seeded fresh long red chili peppers
- 2 Peeled and garlic cloves
- 1 Inch of peeled ginger
- ½ Cup of water
- ½ Cup of apple cider vinegar
- ½ cup of mild honey
- 1 Pinch of salt to taste

Instructions

1. Place the chili peppers, the garlic cloves and the ginger in a food processor and process your ingredients until you get a finely chopped mixture
2. Press the setting sauté and let stand until you see the Display HOT
3. Add in the chili mixture, the water, the vinegar and he honey and mix very well to combine
4. Cook while stirring for about 15 to 20 minutes
5. Season with salt to taste
6. Transfer the sauce to a jar or a container and refrigerate or serve immediately and enjoy!

Nutrition Information

Calories: 37| Fat: 0g | Carbohydrates: 10g| Fiber: 0g |Protein: 0g

Recipe 115: Alfredo Sauce

TIME TO PREPARE
5 minutes

COOK TIME
3 Minutes

SERVING
4 People

Ingredients

- 1/2 stick of butter
- 2 teaspoons of minced garlic
- 3 cups of heavy cream
- 1 cup of chicken broth
- 1 teaspoon of coarse ground garlic salt
- 1 teaspoon of fresh ground pepper
- 1 teaspoon of finely minced parsley
- 2 cups of Parmesan cheese - freshly grated
- 1 heaping Tablespoon of flour

Instructions

1. Turn on the 'SAUTE' setting function on your Instant Pot; then add in the butter and the garlic and sauté for about 2 minutes
2. Turn off the setting sauté; then add in the chicken broth, the cream, the garlic, the salt and the pepper
3. Stir your ingredients altogether; then place the lid on your Instant and lock it in place
4. Make sure the pressure valve is set to 'SEALING' position and set the timer for about 1 minute by pressing the MANUAL setting
5. When the pressure cooking time ends; the timer beeps; carefully turn the valve to VENTING and release the pressure
6. Open the lid of your Instant Pot and stir the cream mixture; then mix the flour with the Parmesan cheese and stir until it melts
7. Add in the finely minced parsley; then let the sauce cool
8. Pour the sauce in a jar; and refrigerate until ready to use

Nutrition Information

Calories: 467| Fat: 45g | Carbohydrates: 7g| Fiber: 0g |Protein: 10g

CHAPTER 116: DESSERTS AND BREAD RECIPES

Recipe 117: Cheese Cake

TIME TO PREPARE:
10 minutes

COOK TIME
35 Minutes

SERVING
5 People

Ingredients

- 16 Oz of Ricotta cheese
- 16 Oz of cream cheese
- 8 Oz of sour cream
- 4 Large eggs
- 2 Tablespoon of corn starch
- 2 Tablespoons of flour
- 1 Tablespoon of vanilla extract
- 2 Cups of crumbled Oreos
- 1 Can of sweetened condensed milk
- 1 Cup of melted chocolate
- 1 Cup of shredded coconut

Instructions

1. Mix altogether the cream cheese and the ricotta cheese.
2. Add in the eggs one by one
3. Sift in the flour and the corn starch; then fold in the sour cream
4. Place the crushed Oreos to the bottom of a spring baking tray that fits your Instant Pot.
5. Pour the mixture into a spring tray
6. Cover the tray with a foil tin and seal it very well
7. Pour 1 cup of water in your Instant Pot and place the Trivet in its place in the bottom
8. Put the tray over the trivet and lock the lid
9. Set the timer to about 35 minutes and the pressure to HIGH
10. When the timer beeps; quick release the pressure and set the cheese cake aside to cool; in the meantime, put 1 can of condensed milk in your Instant Pot; then cover it with water
11. Lock the lid of your Instant Pot and seal the valve
12. Set the timer to about 40 minutes and the pressure to HIGH
13. When the timer beeps; quick release the pressure;

then remove the can aside to cool
14. Spread the caramel over the cheesecake; then coat it with the coconut and the melted chocolate
15. Serve and enjoy your cheesecake!

Nutrition Information

Calories: 163| Fat: 18g | Carbohydrates: 19g| Fiber: 3g |Protein: 4.6g

Recipe 118: Chocolate Cookies

TIME TO PREPARE:
7 minutes

COOK TIME
10 Minutes

SERVING
8 People

Ingredients

- 2 and ¼ cups of tightly packed Almond Flour
- ½ Teaspoon of salt
- ½ Teaspoon of Baking Soda
- 2 Large eggs
- ¼ Cup of Organic Agave Nectar
- 1/3 Cup of Grape Seed Oil
- 1/3 Cup of Dairy Free Chocolate Chips

Instructions

1. Pour 1 cup of water in your Instant Pot
2. Place the trivet in its place in the bottom of your Instant Pot
3. Mix all your ingredients in a large bowl except for the chocolate chips
4. Use a spoon to stir your ingredients
5. Stir in your chocolate chips.
6. Grease a baking tray with cooking spray; then form cookies with a scoop
7. Arrange the cookies over your baking tray and cover the tray with a foil
8. Place the baking tray in the Instant Pot and lock the lid
9. Set the timer to about 10 minutes and the pressure to HIGH
10. When the timer beeps; quick release the pressure
11. Set the cookies aside to cool for about 10 minutes
12. Serve and enjoy your cookies!

Nutrition Information

Calories: 148| Fat: 7.4g | Carbohydrates: 20g| Fiber: 0.6g |Protein: 1.5g

Recipe 119: Brownie Cake

TIME TO PREPARE:
6 minutes

COOK TIME
25 Minutes

SERVING
5 People

Ingredients

- 5 Tablespoons of softened butter
- ¼ Cup of unsweetened cocoa powder
- 1 Cup of sugar
- ¾ Cup of flour
- ¼ Tablespoon of vanilla
- ¾ Teaspoon of baking powder
- 2 Large eggs
- 1 Tablespoon of diced walnuts
- 1 and ½ cups of water
- 1 Tablespoon of creamy peanut butter

Instructions

1. Put your dry ingredients into a bowl and the wet ingredients in another bowl and mix each very well
2. Add all your ingredients together; then toss in the nuts and mix again
3. Grease a baking tray with cooking spray
4. Add the diced walnuts to the mixture and
5. Line the greased baking tray with a parchment paper and put 1 tablespoon of peanut butter right in the middle
6. Pour the batter of your brownie cake in the baking tray and cover it with an aluminum foil
7. Pour 1 and ½ cups of water in the Instant Pot
8. Place the trivet in the bottom of your Instant Pot and place the tray in

9. Lock the lid of the Instant Pot and set the timer to about 25 minutes and the pressure to low
10. When the timer beeps; quick release the pressure; then set the cake aside to cool for about 5 minutes
11. Serve and enjoy your brownie cake!

Nutrition Information

Calories: 112| Fat: 7g | Carbohydrates: 12g| Fiber: 0.0g |Protein: 1.6g

Recipe 120: Coconut Custard

TIME TO PREPARE:
5 minutes

COOK TIME
30 Minutes

SERVING
3 People

Ingredients

- 1 Cup of unsweetened coconut milk
- 3 Large eggs
- 1/3 Cup of maple syrup
- 3 to 4 drops of Pandan extract

Instructions

1. In a bowl; mix the milk with eggs, the sweetener and the extract of Pandan
2. Stir your ingredients very well; then pour the batter into a greased baking ramekin
3. Pour 2 cups of water in your Instant Pot and place the trivet in its place
4. Cove the ramekin with an aluminum foil and place it over the trivet
5. Lock the lid of your Instant Pot and set the timer to about 30 minutes and the pressure to HIGH
6. When the timer beeps; naturally release the pressure
7. Refrigerate the custard; then serve and enjoy it!

Nutrition Information

Calories: 189| Fat: 9.8g | Carbohydrates: 20g| Fiber: 0.2g |Protein: 4.5g

Recipe 121: Chocolate Mousse

TIME TO PREPARE: 5 minutes

COOK TIME 6 Minutes

SERVING 2-3 People

Ingredients

- 1 and ½ cups of heavy cream
- ½ Cup of whole milk
- 5 Egg yolks
- ¼ Cup of sugar
- 1 Pinch of salt
- 8 Ounces of melted bittersweet chocolate
- Grated chocolate

Instructions

1. Pour the milk in a small pan over a medium high heat and let simmer
2. Whisk the eggs yolks with the sugar and the salt
3. Slowly, add in the cream milk and add in the chocolate and mix very well
4. Pour the batter in 6 cups or mason jars
5. Pour 1 and ½ cups of water in your Instant Pot and place the trivet in its place in the bottom
6. Arrange the cups over the trivet and lock the lid of your Instant Pot
7. Set the timer to about 6 minutes and the pressure to HIGH
8. When the timer beeps; naturally release the pressure; then carefully remove the lid
9. Serve and enjoy your chocolate crème!

Nutrition Information

Calories: 75| Fat: 4.5g | Carbohydrates: 9.2g| Fiber: 0g |Protein: 0g

Recipe 123: Strawberry Compote

TIME TO PREPARE:
4 minutes

COOK TIME
3 Minutes

SERVING
3 People

Ingredients

- 1 Pound of trimmed, washed and cut Fresh Strawberries
- 1/8 Cup of Sugar or to taste
- 1 Oz of Fresh Orange Juice
- 1 Pinch of ground ginger
- Vanilla Bean

Instructions

1. Add the strawberries to your Instant Pot
2. Sprinkle a little bit of sugar over the strawberries and set aside for about 10 minutes
3. Squeeze a little bit of orange juice; then lock the lid of your Instant Pot and seal the valve
4. Set the timer to about 3 minutes and the pressure to HIGH
5. When the timer beeps; quick release the pressure
6. Serve and enjoy your compote!

Nutrition Information

Calories: 75| Fat: 4.5g | Carbohydrates: 9.2g| Fiber: 0g |Protein: 0g

Recipe 124: Instant Pot Flan

TIME TO PREPARE:
5 minutes

COOK TIME
5 Minutes

SERVING
4 People

Ingredients

- 4 Large eggs
- 2 Cups of fresh goat cheese
- Around ½ Cup of condensed milk
- 1 Cup of white sugar
- 2 Teaspoons of water

Instructions

1. Start with the caramel; prepare it by heating the sugar with water in your mold.
2. But don't stir too much
3. Once finished, set the caramel aside and take a deep bowl
4. Blend the eggs in the bowl with the condensed milk and the cheese
5. Pour the mixture of eggs into your already caramelized mold (It should be a heat proof mold or a steel one)
6. Cover the mold with foil and place it on the trivet in the Instant Pot after pouring around 1 and ½ cups of water
7. Close the lid and set at high pressure for around 5 minutes
8. Once the timer beeps, quick release the pressure; and after 10 minutes; serve and enjoy a delicious taste.

Nutrition Information

Calories: 221.9| Fat: 6.2g | Carbohydrates: 34.9g| Fiber: 0g |Protein: 6.9g

Recipe 125: Chocolate Cupcakes

TIME TO PREPARE:
10 minutes

COOK TIME
15 Minutes

SERVING
9 People

Ingredients

- 1 and ½ cups of all purpose flour
- 1 Cup of sugar
- ¼ Cup of cocoa powder
- 1/8 teaspoon of Baking soda
- 1 pinch of salt
- 1 teaspoon of vinegar
- 1 and ½ cup of Milk
- 2 Teaspoons of Vanilla extract
- ¼ Cup of water
- ½ Cup of sunflower oil

Instructions

1. Prepare a number of steel small sized tins or small heatproof ramekins and grease them; then set it aside
2. Mix all together the flour, the sugar, the cocoa powder, the salt, the baking soda, the salt and combine the mixture very well
3. In a deep bowl, combine all together the oil and the vinegar and whisk the mixture. Sift in the flour and mix very well.
4. Add the vanilla essence and the water and combine the ingredients very well.
5. Pour the obtained batter into your prepared ramekins and make sure you don't exceed the ¾ full
6. Now, time to heat your Instant Pot
7. Place the Instant Pot over a medium heat and spread salt into the bottom, press sauté for around 5 minutes
8. Once the salt is hot and becomes brown, add a steel plate to separate the salt and line the ramekins on a baking dish; cover it with foil and then place it in the Instant Pot.

9. Switch the heat to medium and bake, with the lid on, for around 15 minutes.
10. Check with a toothpick to see if the cupcakes are fully cooked. Finally, serve and enjoy your cupcakes!

Nutrition Information

Calories: 190| Fat: 11 g | Carbohydrates: 22g| Fiber: 0.5g |Protein: 1g

Recipe 126: Chocolate Chip Cake

TIME TO PREPARE:
7 minutes

COOK TIME
25 Minutes

SERVING
5 People

Ingredients

- 1 and ½ cups of all-purpose flour
- ½ Cup of cocoa
- 1 Teaspoon of ground cinnamon
- ¼ Teaspoon of salt
- ½ Teaspoon of baking soda
- ½ Teaspoon of baking powder
- ½ Cup of soften butter
- 1 Cup of granulated sugar
- 2 large beaten eggs
  ¾ Cup of mini chocolate chips

Instructions

1. In a deep medium bowl, mix all together the flour, the spices, the salt, the baking soda, and the baking powder and set it aside.
2. In a mixing bowl, combine the cream, the sugar and the butter until they become a kind of fluffy.
3. Add one egg at a time and keep mixing.
4. Once you add all the eggs, add your dry ingredients and whisk until you obtain a well mixed mixture
5. Add the chocolate chips, and spoon your batter into a greased heat proof baking dish that fits your Instant Pot.
6. Cover the baking dish with a foil and prepare your Instant Pot by pouring 1 and ½ cups of water in it and fix the trivet right into the bottom of the Instant Pot
7. Close the lid of the Instant Pot and set at high pressure for around 25 minutes
8. When the timer beeps, quick release the pressure
9. Serve and enjoy your cake

Nutrition Information

Calories: 189| Fat: 10g | Carbohydrates: 31g| Fiber: 0.5g |Protein: 4g

RECIPE 127: PEAR COMPOTE

TIME TO PREPARE:
5 minutes

COOK TIME
8 Minutes

SERVING
4 People

Ingredients

- 2 lb of pears
- 1 Cup of Brioche
- ½ Cup of caster sugar
- 1 and ¼ Cup of l water
- 1 Teaspoon of ground ginger

Instructions

1. Start by peeling and coring the pears and cut it into small dices.
2. Now, cut the brioche into small pieces.
3. Prepare your Instant Pot and place it over a medium heat
4. Pour the water into the Instant Pot, the brioche, the sugar and the ginger, then add the pears
5. Close the lid of the Instant Pot for and set at high pressure for around 8 minutes
6. When the timer beeps, quick release the pressure
7. Crush your fruits with a fork and finally, serve and enjoy!

Nutrition Information

Calories: 139| Fat: 0.2g | Carbohydrates: 35.8g| Fiber: 0.0g |Protein: 0.7g

Recipe 128: Strawberry Mousse

TIME TO PREPARE:
5 minutes

COOK TIME
15 Minutes

SERVING
3 People

Ingredients

- 2 Large egg yolks
- 2 Tablespoons of water
- ¼ Cup of Swerve
- ½ Cup of cream
- ¼ Cup of almond milk
- ½ Teaspoon of vanilla
- 5 Strawberries
- 5 Blueberries

Instructions

1. Place the trivet in the bottom of your Instant Pot
2. Pour 1 and ½ cups of water in the Instant
3. In a small pot and over a medium hot stove, mix the water with the swerve and mix very well for about 1 to 2 minutes
4. Remove the pan from the heat and mix the cream with the almond milk and the vanilla
5. Combine the egg yolks and add 1 tablespoon of the mixture of the cream and mix very well
6. Gradually, add the cream into your eggs and don't stop whisking
7. Pour the batter into small greased ramekins and arrange it over the trivet
8. Lock the lid of the Instant Pot and set the timer to about 6 minutes and the pressure to HIGH
9. When the timer beeps; quick release the pressure; then let the ramekins refrigerate for about 15 minutes
10. Top the ramekins with strawberry slices
11. Serve and enjoy your delicious Mousse!

Nutrition Information

Calories: 139| Fat: 0.2g | Carbohydrates: 35.8g| Fiber: 0.0g |Protein: 0.7g

RECIPE 129: CRÈME BRULE

TIME TO PREPARE: 7minutes

COOK TIME 7 Minutes

SERVING 4 People

Ingredients

- 8 Yolks of eggs
- 1/3 Cup of granulated sugar
- ½ Teaspoon of salt
- 2 Cups of heavy cream
- 1 and ½ teaspoons of vanilla
- 6 Tbsp of superfine sugar

Instructions

1. Place your Instant Pot over a medium heat and pour 1 and ½ cups of cold water in it.
2. Place the trivet into its place in the bottom of the Instant Pot
3. In a deep bowl, combine all together, the eggs yolks, 1/3 cup of the granulated sugar with 1 pinch of salt and whisk very well.
4. Add the cream and the vanilla and mix until the ingredients become very well combined
5. Pour the spout into the mixture
6. Pour your obtained batter into 6 heat proof ramekins
7. Cover the ramekins with foil and line it n the trivet in your Instant Pot.
8. Close the lid of the Instant Pot and set at high pressure for around 7 minutes
9. When the timer beeps, quick release the pressure

and refrigerate your ramekins
10. Serve with a sprinkle of sugar powder top with crispy walnuts

Nutrition Information

Calories: 343| Fat: 22g | Carbohydrates: 27g| Fiber: 0.0g |Protein: 3g

Recipe 130: Sweet Cinnamon Almonds

TIME TO PREPARE:
5 minutes

COOK TIME
18 Minutes

SERVING
3 People

Ingredients

- 1 and ½ cups of sugar
- 1 and ½ cups of light brown sugar
- 3 Tablespoons of cinnamon
- 1/8 Teaspoon of salt
- 1 Large egg white
- 2 Teaspoons of vanilla
- 4 and ½ cups of almonds
- ¼ Cup of water

Instructions

1. Spray your Instant Pot with a non stick cooking spray; then set it aside
2. In a large and deep bowl, mix the cinnamon with the sugar and the salt; then stir very well
3. In a separate bowl; mix the egg white with the vanilla and stir very well until your mixture becomes frothy
4. Place the almonds in the mixture of the eggs and toss very well; then pour the almonds into the mixture of the sugar and mix again.
5. Pour your mixture in your instant pot, Electric pressure cooker and lock the lid
6. Set the timer to about 18 minutes and the pressure to HIGH
7. When the timer beeps; quick release the pressure
8. Line a baking tray with a parchment paper and let it cool for about 10 minutes
9. Serve and enjoy your almonds!

Nutrition Information

Calories: 16| Fat: 0.6g | Carbohydrates: 2.4g| Fiber: 0.1g |Protein: 0.4g

Recipe 131: Apple Cinnamon Rolls

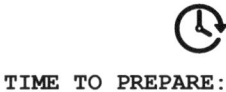

TIME TO PREPARE:
5 minutes

COOK TIME
18 Minutes

SERVING
3 People

Ingredients

- 2 Cans of Pillsbury Cinnamon Rolls
- 4 peeled and chopped green apples
- ¾ Cup of sugar
- 1½ Teaspoons of ground cinnamon
- ½ Cup of melted

Instructions

1. Mix the sugar and the cinnamon all together and make sure that the ingredients are very well combined.
2. Peel all of your apples and chop it into dices.
3. Separate the cinnamon rolls and put the icing to its side.
4. Cut into the shape of pies and toss the cinnamon rolls and the apples with the cinnamon sugar and the butter
5. Pour a cup of water into your Instant Pot and pour all of your ingredients into baking pan of a spring form
6. Place the baking dish on the trivet and close the lid of your Instant Pot and set at high pressure for around 20 minutes
7. Once the timer beeps, quick release the pressure and set it aside to cool down for around 10 minutes
8. Once it is cool, flip your baking dish into a large serving plate

9. Pour the icing over the top of your bread and serve
10. Enjoy a delicious taste

Nutrition Information

Calories: 16| Fat: 0.6g | Carbohydrates: 2.4g| Fiber: 0.1g |Protein: 0.4g

Recipe 132: Pecan Pie

TIME TO PREPARE: 8 minutes

COOK TIME 25 Minutes

SERVING 4-5 People

Ingredients

- ¾ cup of All Purpose Flour
- ½ tsp of Baking Soda
- 2/3 cup of Brown Sugar
- ¼ cup of Powdered Buttermilk
- 1 tbsp of cinnamon
- 2 Beaten Eggs
- ½ melted stick of Butter
- ¾ cup of chopped Pecans
- 1 can of Cinnamon Roll Icing; optional
- ½ cup of chopped Pecans (garnish)
- 1 can of Olive Oil Baking Spray

Instructions

1. Spray a baking cake pan with a non-stick spray.
2. Pour ½ cup of water into your Instant Pot and place a trivet over the water
3. In a large bowl; mix the flour with the buttermilk powder, the baking soda, the salt, and the brown sugar
4. Once mixed; add in the eggs, the melted butter, and the pecans.
5. Scoop the batter in the prepared cake pan; then place the pan on top of the trivet on your Instant pot and seal the lid
6. Cook on High pressure for about 25 minutes; then let the pressure naturally release
7. Carefully remove the pan; then let cool for about 10 minutes before inverting the cake from the pan to a plate
8. Top the cake with the whipped icing and the pecans.
9. Serve and enjoy your cake!

- ½ cup of water

Nutrition Information

Calories: 502| Fat: 27.1g | Carbohydrates: 63.7g| Fiber: 4.3g |Protein: 6g

Recipe 133: Lava Cake

TIME TO PREPARE: 10 minutes

COOK TIME 12 Minutes

SERVING 3 People

Ingredients

- 2 ½ cups of self Raising Flour
- 1 ½ cups of Butter
- 1 ¼ cup of Caster Sugar
- 2 ½ cups of organic Cocoa Powder
- 1 Cup of Dark Chocolate
- 2 Large Eggs
- 30 ml of Whole Milk
- 1 Tbsp of Vanilla Essence
- 1 Handful of Fresh Raspberries

Instructions

1. Start by greasing a large mixing bowl
2. In the mixing bowl; add the butter and the sugar; then the cream the fat into the sugar.
3. Beat in the eggs once at a time until the mixture is very well mixed
4. Add in the milk, the cocoa powder and the vanilla; then add a little quantity of flour, about hakf the quantity of the flour
5. Mix your ingredients very well; then fold in the remaining flour
6. Place some squares of the chocolate into your mixture until you get the chocolate melted
7. Pour 1 cup of water into your Instant Pot; then place the steaming rack over the water; then place the mixing bowl
8. Cover the Instant Pot with the lid; then move to

sealing position and seal the valve
9. Cook for about 12 minutes on the function "Steam"
10. When completely done; you will hear six beeps
11. Unseal the valve and once the steam is completely released; open it up; then serve and enjoy your chocolate lava cake with fresh chopped raspberries!

Nutrition Information

Calories: 649| Fat: 35g | Carbohydrates: 82g| Fiber: 6g |Protein: 13g

CONCLUSION

"The Ultimate Instant Pot cookbook 2020"

Not only this cook book has offered you some of the most delicious Instant Pot Recipes that you can ever find; but it also includes very helpful information that will help you professionally use your Instant Pot Electric Pressure cookers even if this is your first time using an electric pressure cooker. So, with the help this Electric Pressure cookbook, you will be able to learn some of the most important benefits, function and even tips of Instant Pot use, Electric Pressure cookers.

Therefore, if you have a busy lifestyle this cookbook will be your guide; as it will save, both, your time and money. In this book; you will learn to cook a wide variety of healthy breakfast, meat, poultry, bread and even dessert recipes. And what makes the recipes you will find in this book the best and the healthiest amongst many others, is that all the ingredients are simple and affordable to all users as well as healthy as possible. You will be amazed at how fast Electric Pressure Cooking is and what is more important is that Instant Pot, Electric Pressure Cookers will help you maintain the same delicious taste your love with a super tender taste.

Instant Pots can also help you enjoy the juiciness of meat in your meals in a matter of a few minutes. Using an Instant Pot, Electric Pressure Cooker will help you pressure cook a proper meal to enjoy it with your friends, family and can even cook on special occasions. And even if you are adopting a healthy lifestyle and a special diet; you can rely on this book because it will show you how to cook in an Instant Pot with simple directions and you will also find all the nutrition information of each recipe. So, if you are a new user of Instant Pot, Electric Pressure Cookers; this cook book will be of a great use to you; so what are you waiting for to purchase your own copy of this Instant Pot Cookbook.

And even you have any concerns or doubt about using Instant Pots, Electric Pressure Cookers; please; don't hesitate reading this cookbook because it won't leave any doubts and it will provide you with the information that can help you master the use of your cooking appliance properly. Get ready because this Electric Pressure Cooker cookbook will offer you a wide range of extremely healthy and creative recipes that you will be able to cook like a Master Chef. You will get addicted to the sumptuous taste of our elevated recipes and you will be able to discover some of the most innovative cooking techniques that you will not be able to resist.

Thank you for Reading the Ultimate Instant Pot cookbook 2020"

We are extremely happy have been able to offer you this Instant Pot, Electric Pressure Cooker cookbook and we hope that you have benefited from it and enjoyed it. And please, do not hesitate to share this cookbook with your friends or to offer it as a gift for your sister, mother or any of your acquaintances. We care about you and your health and we have tried to offer you an exciting cooking journey. And our dear readers, we are looking forward to any suggestions that will help us continue our work.

Printed in Great Britain
by Amazon